MW00570543

# Out of the Flames

## Fires and Fire Fighting
## on the Canadian Prairies

### Faye Reineberg Holt

FIFTH
HOUSE
PUBLISHERS

Front cover painting, "The Fire Guard," 1923 by Inglis Sheldon Williams. Oil on canvas, 66.00 x 88.9 cm. Collection of the MacKenzie Art Gallery, Regina, Saskatchewan. Gift of Mr. Norman MacKenzie. Photo: Don Hall. Back cover image courtesy Western Canadian Pictorial Index.
Cover and interior design by John Luckhurst / GDL.

The publisher gratefully acknowledges the support of The Canada Council for the Arts and the Department of Canadian Heritage for our publishing program.

THE CANADA COUNCIL | LE CONSEIL DES ARTS
FOR THE ARTS | DU CANADA
SINCE 1957 | DEPUIS 1957

We acknowledge the financial support of the Government of Canada through the Book Publishing Industry Development Program for our publishing activities.

Printed in Canada.

98 99 00 01 02 / 5 4 3 2 1

CANADIAN CATALOGUING IN PUBLICATION DATA
Reineberg Holt, Faye.
    Out of the flames

    Includes bibliographical references and index.
    ISBN 1-894004-14-0

1. Fire extinction–Prairie Provinces–History.
2. Fire extinction–Prairie Provinces–Anecdotes. I. Title.
TH9506.P7R44 1998    363.37'8'09712    C98-910742-6

Fifth House Ltd.
#9 - 6125 11 St. SE
Calgary, AB, Canada
T2H 2L6
1-800-360-8826

# Table of Contents

## Dedication

To my mother, Ruby Reineberg, who, as a young girl,
sat on a hill and watched as the flames of a prairie fire
turned the sky a glowing red. With my thanks and love.

## Acknowledgements

Special thanks to my ever-patient husband, my editor,
Liesbeth Leatherbarrow, Archie McAllister, Tom McCarty,
Fred Yellow Old Woman, the librarians and archivists of the
Glenbow Museum, other museums cited, and the RCMP
Retired Veterans Association and Museum.

*This was a familiar scene as Winnipeg firemen rushed
from the firehall to respond to yet another emergency.*
Western Canadian Pictorial Index A0526-16793

# Introduction

> The grandeur of the prairie on fire belongs
> to itself. It is like a volcano in full activity, you
> cannot imitate it, because it is impossible to
> obtain those gigantic elements from which it
> derives its awful splendour.
>
> *Henry Youle Hind, 1858[1]*

Since the days of early human development, fire has symbolized hearth, home, and survival. In the Canadian West, where winter weather can be merciless, fire has meant the difference between life and death. It has also been an enemy more fearsome than winter's icy blizzards and frigid temperatures. From early spring until fall, no phenomenon has more frequently created awe and terror in the West than yellow, orange, and red flames racing across the landscape.

In the central, northern, and mountain regions of the prairie provinces, forest fires are the enemy. Often studied, these fires ravage vast stands of timber and nearby communities. In the more heavily populated central parkland and southern plains of the prairies, grass fires threaten towns and cities, level farms, and char endless stretches of crop and pastureland.

The frequency and magnitude of parkland and plains fires have affected prairie people deeply. Embedded in their collective subconscious, these prairie fires have almost mythic significance for Westerners.

*Prairie*, the French word for fields, was used by early explorers to describe the rolling savannahs and semi-treed areas they found in the central regions of what are now Alberta, Saskatchewan, and Manitoba. The open country consisted of long grass and meadows, small trees and bushes, and sloughs and hills, which reminded them of the fields of home. They found similar conditions in some northern areas, such as Grand Prairie,

1

*This small wagon train travelled through the prairie fertile belt en route from Fort Vermilion to Wainwright, Alberta. Although poplar groves, tall grass, and a hilly landscape provided suitable conditions and plenty of fuel for large prairie fires, the conditions were somewhat less hazardous than on the plains to the south, where very strong winds were also common.*
Glenbow Archives NA-424-26

Alberta. This prairie landscape, often referred to as parkland or the fertile belt, has been the scene of thousands of fires.

The fires that loom largest in the memories of Westerners are those that raged on the southern plains. Stretching across the three prairie provinces and into the United States, the Great Plains constitutes the worst natural fire belt in the Canadian West.

To early settlers, the fertile parklands and arid plains became known as the land of prairie fires. The uniqueness of the geographical region was first defined by Captain James Palliser. In 1857, he headed a British expedition instructed to report on conditions in the West. Palliser identified one large, triangle-shaped area as unfit for settlement and agriculture. He called it the central desert, but it is now known as the Palliser Triangle. In Canada, the triangle is bounded on the south by the international border along the forty-ninth parallel, extending from 100° to 114° west longitude; its apex terminates at 52° north latitude.[2]

It is impossible to determine how many fires have plagued the Palliser Triangle over the years. Early official reports by the North-West Mounted Police make frequent references to fires. However, the systematic gathering of fire statistics is a reasonably recent development. Many local fire departments have collected statistics for the towns they serve, but they have seldom documented fires on distant farms, in fields, and on wild lands. Forest fire statistics are readily available for economic reasons, and some national and provincial statistics also exist. However, no data have been collected for the area encompassed by the Palliser Triangle itself.

Fortunately, a study on natural fire cycles in some of the national parks was carried out in the 1980s, and it gives an idea of how serious the problem of fire is for the Palliser Triangle, compared to other parts of the country.[3] Natural fire cycles are estimated in years; the shorter the fire cycle, the more frequent the fires in an area. It is not always possible to determine whether fires were started by people or lightning, so the study did not differentiate on that basis.

Grasslands National Park, located in southwest Saskatchewan in the Palliser Triangle, covered 142 square kilometres (55 square miles) at the time of the study.[4] Results indicated that the park had a natural fire cycle ranging from one to twenty-five years. The small national historic parks of Batoche

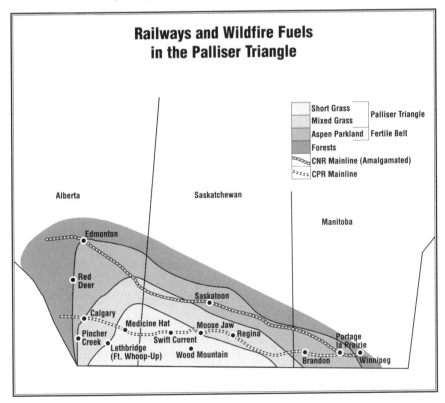

Railways and Wildfire Fuels
in the Palliser Triangle

*This lightning storm occurred at Suffield, Alberta. From 1925 to 1934, light-*
*ning caused fifteen percent of the wildfires in Canada; from 1951 to 1960,*
*twenty-two percent; and in 1961, thirty-three percent. The apparent increase*
*in fires caused by lightning is the result of fewer railway and settler-related*
*fires.* Medicine Hat Museum and Art Gallery PC581.81

---

and Fort Walsh, also in the Palliser Triangle, were characterized by the same, short natural fire cycle, meaning they experienced frequent fires.

The fire history was also recorded for 525.8 square kilometres (203 square miles) in Alberta's Waterton National Park, which is part grassland and part foothills. The results showed that about six percent of the park had a natural fire cycle of one to twenty-five years; about half had a fire cycle of more than a hundred years.

These results are in marked contrast with results from parks in other parts of Canada. For example, none of the national parks in Quebec had a natural fire cycle of less than one hundred years, indicating fires were much less frequent there than in the Palliser Triangle. Similarly, most Ontario national parks showed natural fire cycles of fifty years, or longer. In the Atlantic region, well over half the land in national parks had a fire cycle of more than three hundred years.

The parklands and plains of the prairies have a climate and geography that are ideal for the spread of fire. The threat of fire peaks in the spring and again in the fall. In this region of stark contrasts, the fire season can also be extended by periodic Chinooks and mild winters.

The annual precipitation in the Palliser Triangle is scant, which increases the risk of fire. Normally, the plains and parkland receive up to 45 centimetres (18 inches) of precipitation a year, but actual amounts vary across the prairies. Winnipeg, Manitoba, averages as much as 53 centimetres (21 inches) per year, while Saskatoon, Saskatchewan, and Medicine Hat, Alberta, only receive about 35 centimetres (14 inches) per year.[5]

This is a land where fire bolts from the sky cause fires. Today, modern high-tech equipment monitors lightning strikes. In a twenty-four-hour period beginning 19 May 1998, Alberta Environment reported about five thousand lightning bolts within the province. Much-needed rain had just fallen, which reduced the fire risk. Nevertheless, lightning sparked twenty fires that day.[6]

Summers in the Palliser Triangle are not only dry but also hot, sucking up what little moisture exists. During July, for example, the mean daily maximum temperatures are 27.7°C (82°F) in much of southern Saskatchewan.[7]

Worse yet, the land of fire is also the land of ruthless, drying winds, especially in southern Alberta. In winter, Chinook winds devour what little

*The original fire engine in Lacombe, Alberta, was made by the Burris Company and nicknamed "The Burper." The town was proud of its early fire department, which won three trophies during fire-fighting competitions in Calgary.* Glenbow Archives NA-1583-7

protective covering snow offers, leaving the previous year's vegetation as dry kindling for hungry flames. Winds can reach gale-force strength and cause fires to spread at tremendous speeds, over unbelievable distances. At Lethbridge, Alberta, the wind seems never-ending, and there, perhaps more than any other factor, wind has orchestrated the spread of fires.

On the southern plains, there are few natural barriers to halt fires. Even though the North and South Saskatchewan Rivers are wide, large fires have leaped them. Many other rivers offer little more than a skip and a jump to flames. Although the plains are flat, the parklands are slightly hilly, and there, fires follow their natural preference of running uphill. Once the country bursts into flame, the elemental force of fire has the perfect landscape for running wild.

The wildfires of the prairies have threatened everyone and everything in their paths. Attempting to escape, hundreds of animals have hurried ahead of flames, including massive herds of buffalo, bounding antelope, and loping coyotes. Smaller scurrying animals, such as gophers and slow-moving porcupine, have had little chance of escaping. For the animals that survived, their blackened homeland provided neither food nor shelter for long periods of time, although eventually it returned to its earlier abundance.

New fire-fighting techniques have tempered human fear. Technological progress may even have lulled some Westerners into feeling safe from their old enemy, but the fires have relinquished none of their power. A glimpse of billowing smoke miles away, or of a dancing wildfire nearby, quickly rekindles old fears.

Yet, fire has also been the source of unparalleled and terrifying beauty, lighting up prairie horizons with fiery red flames. Of course, the story of prairie fire has much in common with the history of fire and fire fighting elsewhere in the world. Nevertheless, there are aspects that are unique to the prairie fires of the Canadian West. Both in the past and the present, these infernos have transformed the landscape, created victims, and made heroes. They have become part of the identity of Westerners. The stories of fires are the stories of people struggling individually and as a group against an awe-inspiring enemy.

# CHAPTER ONE

# Land of Fire

Prairie fires have a past as long as the history of the prairie itself. Firestorms ignited by lightning have always raced across parkland and plains. Other conflagrations have been the result of people's carelessness. At times, fire has been a friendly ally to prairie inhabitants, but capricious and fickle, flames have also quickly turned on friends.

The great infernos on the Canadian prairies have treated everyone equally. From earliest times, Native people knew their home was a land of fire. Then, during the eighteenth and nineteenth centuries, traders, explorers, missionaries, and adventurers also were terrorized by fire. Dancing and racing with the wind, flames drove animals from the area and left a charred landscape where survival was uncertain.

People newly arrived on the prairies often came from countries where fire was not an enormous risk. When flames swept around them, they wondered who caused the fires. Many blamed the indigenous people. They assumed the wildfires were purposefully set to devastate an enemy or to encourage the growth of lush native grasses the following year. They also assumed infernos were sparked by Native carelessness. The idea that lightning was a significant natural cause for fire on the prairies was seldom considered. Many newcomers also did not acknowledge that their own campfires or carelessness could, and did, spark numerous fires, given the windy and dry conditions of their new land. As a result, what was truth and what was falsehood often became blurred when it came to laying blame for prairie fires.

## Smoke and Mirrors

The earliest history of prairie fires exists within the oral, story-telling tradition and the myths of the prairie's first people: Assiniboine, Cree, Sioux, Blackfoot, and Sarcee. The most direct tie between the great fires and the

Native people can be made with the Blackfoot Confederacy, which includes the Siksikah or Blackfoot (proper), the Kainai or Blood, and the Peigan.

The people known to explorers, traders, and early settlers as Blackfoot called themselves *soyi-tapix*, the Prairie People, or the People Whose Moccasins Were Blackened by Prairie Fire. Their territory was the area of the prairies most often prey to fire. According to tradition, a Native traveller visiting from the north bestowed the name *soyi-tapix*. To those who later explored and settled in Canada, this was translated as *Blackfoot*, and to those in the United States, as *Blackfeet*.

According to Fred Yellow Old Woman, a Blackfoot translator, historian, and linguist, fire was one of the four elements of life for Native people. Water, grass, air, and fire were all sacred. If any one of them was out of balance, it was not good for the people, so they strived to keep them in harmony.

Year after year, the First Nations people saw the devastation fire could bring, yet they needed fire to survive. From time immemorial, aboriginal people had used fire as a tool for warmth and cooking. Usually, their fires were small, smaller than those of the explorers, hunters, and traders who came later. On the Great Plains, where fuel was precious, Native people learned the art and science of concentrating, conserving, and controlling heat by using dirt berms around fires and rocks beneath them to hold heat. Controlled and extinguished, their fires posed minimal risk to the prairies.

Indians had other uses for fires, too, uses that newcomers seldom understood. In a time before telegraph, telephone, and e-mail, the sun flashing on mirrors and signal fires carried messages about the location of buffalo, the intrusion of visitors, and the safe arrival of Native travellers at their destinations. Although their smoke was visible for vast distances, the fires were small and well controlled. The Native expression for these signal fires was *putting out fire*. Ironically, today the same English expression means to extinguish flames rather than to place fire out on the prairie.

Prior to the 1700s, before horses and rifles were available for hunting, Native people used fire to herd and turn the buffalo. The responsibility for this job lay with the scouts who were experts both with buffalo and fire. When the animals were still days away from the pounds and jumps where they would be slaughtered, the scouts, disguised as buffalo calves or wolves, used the animals' fear of fire to affect their movements. For this, small, well-placed fires were essential tools.

Even after the arrival of horses made hunting easier, scouts continued to use the same techniques to herd buffalo. Once they sighted a herd, they

*Massive buffalo herds, essential to the survival of plains Indians, would temporarily disappear from lands blackened by fire, causing hardship and starvation in Native communities.* Whyte Museum of the Canadian Rockies V527/PS-648

would head to the highest ground, where wind could play a critical role in spreading flames. The scouts would then take hair from their hide clothing, hold it above their heads, and release it, to determine the wind direction. If the wind was right, the scouts would light a fire and then work like cowboys, gathering and herding as the animals scattered in response to their natural instinct to avoid smoke.

Because the scouts were careful and aware of the risks, their fires seldom became wildfires. However, indigenous people did use planned burns to keep their world in balance. According to Yellow Old Woman, they were not often caught by fires on the wide-open prairie, because they were always on the move, and their villages were located in the relatively safe zones along rivers.

Too much vegetation in the valleys, however, sometimes caused problems for Natives. Waist-high grass and heavy layers of matted grass and broken branches impeded their progress through low-lying areas near the rivers and creeks. In addition, new grass, essential for feeding horses and buffalo, did not grow well where deep mats of mouldy pasture had accumulated for decades or even centuries. Finally, mosquitoes abounded in the wet, mossy, low-lying areas. Under these circumstances, the four elements of life—water, grass, air, and fire—were not in harmony.

To correct the resultant imbalance, Natives would plan controlled burns, just as settlers planned burns to clear land and destroy weed patches. According to Yellow Old Woman, there was "an official way of doing it ... They had a big ceremony, and said this is good when there is no wind."[1]

The relationships between fire, buffalo, and the First Nations people were seldom as simple as newcomers assumed. Natives, explorers, and traders agreed that the year following a fire, grass grew lush and green, enticing the buffalo to their hunting grounds. To that end, controlled burns were useful for Natives, but wildfires were another matter. Very hot wildfires killed grass roots; overgrazing during the first year after a severe fire also killed grass roots. To aboriginal people, damaged grass meant the four elements of life were again out of balance. In practical terms, it meant that the prairies could support fewer animals after a severe wildfire than before, thus diminishing the Native food supply.

Newcomers also didn't acknowledge other problems in the complex relationship between Natives and fire. On the treeless plains of the southern prairies, buffalo chips were the only available fuel for cooking fires. Prairie fire that blackened vast landscapes also devoured the buffalo chips that Indian people needed to survive the winter.

The earliest written records concerning Native use of fire are found in the journals of explorers, fur traders, and missionaries. During his journey to the Canadian West between 1857 and 1858, Henry Youle Hind was perplexed by his observations. In the hollows of hills on one side of the Saskatchewan River grew young aspen and a few oaks. On the other side, the hills were bare, and the grass was very short. After he learned that Indians often camped and travelled on the short-grass side, he surmised that fire had played a part in the evolution of this area. The fires

> ... are caused by Indians, chiefly for the purpose of telegraphic communication, or to divert the buffalo from the course they may be taking. These operations will cease as the Indians and buffalo diminish, events which are taking place with great rapidity.[2]

With little understanding of aboriginal practices regarding fire, most explorers, including Hind, believed Indians were destroying the prairie with fire. According to Hind, Native carelessness had caused the extension of the barren plains south of Fort Qu'Appelle. He maintained that, as long as Native people lived on the plains and prairie, uncontrolled fires would continue.

Their pretext for putting out fire are so numerous, and their characteristic indifference ... to the results of a conflagration in driving away or destroying the wild animals, so thoroughly a part of their nature, that the annual burning of the prairie may be looked for as a matter of course as long as wild Indians live in the country.[3]

In fact, the consequence of uncontrolled fire on the prairies was even more devastating to Native people than to the newcomers. A village could not be packed and moved quickly enough to avoid destruction when fire, carried by the wind, spread faster than a person could run. Children and adults died. Horses and dogs were destroyed. Some game—the source of food, clothing, bone tools, parfleche goods, and tepee covers—fell victim to flames; other game left the area to escape the flames and in search of food. To Native people, the loss of game and horses for hunting meant starvation. Without game, they also had nothing left to barter for food and other trade goods.

Fire could be friend or enemy. At times, it was a gift from the Great Spirit, a tool Native people could control. At other times, it was a threatening and uncontrollable element in their lives. So, fire always had to be kept in balance with the other elements of life, for the good of the people. Natives believed the Great Spirit would punish them if they did anything to damage Mother Earth and upset that balance.

## Fur Traders, Explorers, and Infernos

Even before Henry Youle Hind set foot in the Canadian West, other newcomers had recorded their experiences with fire on the prairies. Most fur trade posts were built along the rivers of the fertile belt or farther north. There, unlike on the Great Plains, rain and heavy snows helped reduce fire risk. Still, the fur traders watched as fires blackened vast landscapes and threatened lives; and sometimes, they were too close to simply watch the boiling smoke of prairie fires.

Peter Fidler, a Hudson's Bay Company (HBC) employee, was one of western Canada's greatest early explorers, surveyors, and mapmakers. On 16 April 1793, he was camped along the Saskatchewan River when his campfire sparked the nearby grass. With the fire instantly raging out of control, Fidler fled for his life. Leaving behind his equipment, he saddled his horse and raced ahead of the pursuing flames.

On 13 April 1793, every available man at Buckingham House, in the Saskatchewan district near present-day Battleford, had to serve as a fire fighter. They fought a blaze that threatened the HBC post and canoes.

Trader William Tomison blamed his rival, Angus Shaw, for setting the fire. Tomison claimed that Shaw, a trader for the North-West Company (NWC) at Fort George, would do anything to devastate Tomison's trade. Anything, accused Tomison, including firing the prairie.

Fur traders might name their competitors as responsible for causing fires, but more frequently, they blamed Native people. When fire broke out near Fort George about a year and a half later, the NWC clerk, Duncan McGillivray, wrote:

> The Plains around us are all fire. We hear that the animals fly away in every direction to save themselves from the flames, an attempt which is often rendered abortive when the fire is cherished by a breeze of wind, which drives it along with such fury that the fleetest horse can scarcely outrun it. The Indians often make use of this method to frighten away the animals in order to enhance the value of their own provisions.[4]

First Nations people were still being blamed for prairie fires long after the buffalo had disappeared and when fur-bearing animals were no longer the mainstay of prairie economics. However, the people who likely endured the worst tragedies during centuries of prairie infernos were those named for moccasins blackened by the fires. For the most part, the stories of their tragedies remain shrouded in the smoky past, seldom acknowledged in written history. However, in the spring of 1798, the area near Edmonton House experienced its second wildfire in two years, and finally, someone noted Native victims. At least eight had died in the ten-day fire. During the fall of 1812, traders reported that eleven Blackfoot were "consumed in the flames" near the Vermilion River.[5]

James Bird, Chief Factor at Edmonton House, suggested many of the fires in 1812 threatened the survival of Natives and traders alike. For days, an October fire had raged near the fort. The weather was hot and dry, and heavy smoke obscured the sun. It was the worst fire experienced by traders since they had reached the area. Only rain could stop the conflagration; when showers were slow to develop, there was widespread devastation.

Usually, the local Indians traded game for other goods, but after fire had blackened the land from Edmonton to the banks of the South Saskatchewan River, the buffalo disappeared. The Indians found themselves short of food and with nothing to trade. That winter, the men at the HBC post had to find their own food, and out of necessity, Bird sent men to fish more than 80 kilometres (50 miles) away. For everyone, starvation loomed. In the spring of 1813, visitors to Edmonton House circulated stories about the disappearance of the buffalo and widespread hunger. Even at Carlton House in far-off Saskatchewan, the HBC post had inadequate provisions and Natives were starving.

By the end of September 1813, still another fire flared near Edmonton, on the north side of the Saskatchewan River. There, where the parkland blended into forest, the conflagration raged until mid-October. It was finally extinguished by rain and snow, but once again, food was scarce.

## The Palliser Triangle of Fire

Captain John Palliser was one of the first to extensively document the dry climate of the southern prairies. The British expedition, led by Palliser, was organized to determine the suitability of the West for agriculture.

While travelling through the prairies, Captain Palliser and his men witnessed many fires. On 3 October 1857, after watching flames rage near the Red Deer Lakes area, Palliser noted in his diary that the spark from a pipe could set 518 square kilometres (200 square miles) ablaze. Like Henry Youle Hind, who was conducting similar explorations for Canada at the time, Palliser blamed Indians. According to him, they "frequently fire the prairie for the most trivial reasons ... for signals to telegraph one another concerning a successful horse-stealing exploit, or in order to proclaim the safe return of a war party."[6] However, they were "punished," since the fires cut off the buffalo from their area and caused "privation and distress."

Ironically, the next day, Palliser had to admit his own expedition's campfire had run after breakfast. To fight it, the men beat at the flames with bedding and saddle blankets.

Then, on 4 October, Palliser's party observed yet another fire. As a result, they travelled little, setting up camp in a swamp to be safe from flames. That evening, the wind's strength reached gale force. The huge fire had created its own winds, which raged around them. The next morning, the group travelled 16 kilometres (10 miles) across charred ground. Finally, finding a stagnant marsh, the men stopped for breakfast, and their horses grazed the only grass for miles. It was an additional day's travel before they left the blackened landscape.

The reprieve from fire was temporary. Soon they reached another area devastated by fire, between the North and South Saskatchewan Rivers. The long journey had wreaked havoc on the horses' hooves. With soot worsening the horses' condition, the party moved slowly. On 8 October, they reached Fort Carlton. Most of the men wintered there, but Palliser and a small group returned to the Red River Settlement.

On 13 October, nearing a campsite, Palliser discovered the cause of the huge conflagration that had threatened his party. "It was kindled from the campfire of Mons. La Combe [Father Lacombe], the Roman Catholic missionary to the Crees, on his way to Edmonton; this I have learned from a notice planted there, in the shape of a post, on which he carved his initials and the date of the encampment in September."

While Palliser returned to the Red River, Dr. James Hector, another member of the party, remained at Fort Carlton and scouted the area. On 24 October, he was "enveloped in dense masses of smoke, which rolled in volumes from the west, where the woods seemed to be on fire." He didn't know the cause, and his party made it safely back to their encampment. Nevertheless, he sank into a dismal gloom that was difficult to shake. The same feeling would affect thousands of prairie people when they realized the land was burning and they were helpless to stop the devastation.

On 4 March 1859, Hector recorded a smouldering coal bed near the Pembina River, and he surmised it had burned for years. Earlier, he had observed smouldering coal along the Red Deer River. Although the prairies looked like fields of grass, buried beneath the surface and floating on sloughs were fossil fuels that could feed prairie fires and keep them burning, seemingly without end.

In his final report, Palliser suggested that the central desert area of the prairies was not suitable for agriculture. In the central parkland to the north, he noted that annual fires had improved conditions for settlers. By pushing back the northern forests, the fires had reduced the amount of land that needed clearing.

Neither Palliser nor Hind explored the location of present-day Swift Current, Saskatchewan. However, both described the large triangular region that has Swift Current at its centre. Known today as the Palliser Triangle, this is the area in Canada most identified with prairie fires.

## Adventurers

At the same time that traders, explorers, and missionaries were discovering the power of prairie conflagrations, early adventurers and travellers also experienced the wonder and terror of a land on fire. In 1859 and 1860, the Scottish Earl of Southesk travelled in Canada with George Simpson, governor of the Hudson's Bay Company, and his party. When he set out, the earl knew the Canadian West offered supreme hunting and healthful air, but he did not realize the danger lurking in the grass. After crossing the Little Red River, he discarded the match he had used for lighting his pipe. He wrote:

… in an instant the prairie was in a blaze. The wind speedily bore the flames away from us, and ere long the conflagration raged far and wide. I never heard to what extent it spread, but hours afterwards we could see its lurid glow illuminating the darkness of the distant horizon.[7]

Later, at Fort Qu'Appelle and then at the Old Bow Fort, the Earl of Southesk lamented the lack of trees. He admitted the parkland provided pleasant, shady groves, but he claimed the southern plains had been denuded by fire. There, only a sea of grass greeted travellers.

The Earl of Southesk wasn't the first to assume fire had created the barren landscape of the Palliser Triangle, and certainly recurring fires kept the land treeless. However, in 1873, adventurer and explorer Sir William Francis Butler spoke of the plains in terms of their unique beauty. The Palliser Triangle offered

an unending vision of sky and grass, the dim, distant, and ever-shifting horizon; the ridges that seem to be rolled upon one another in motionless torpor; … the sigh and sound of a breeze that seems an echo in unison with the solitude of which it is the sole voice; and above all, the sense of lonely, unending distance.[8]

Still, always lurking in the midst of this seemingly tranquil and idyllic world was the ancient enemy, the fire demon.

# CHAPTER TWO

# *Lurking Enemies*

The prairies' first serious fire fighters, the North-West Mounted Police, were part of a scenario involving buffalo, Native people, and whisky traders. By the 1870s, the Hudson's Bay Company employed dry traders; exchanging whisky for goods was no longer permitted. However, others still bartered for firewater, creating a milieu in which man-caused wildfires were common. The resulting conflagrations threatened people's safety and property, so many Natives, Mounties, surveyors, and settlers made an effort to fight the infernos. Still, they often watched their land, forts, equipment, and homes go up in flames. In the midst of the raging fires, some people became heroes, others victims, and still others villains.

## *Firewater, Wolfers, and Fire*

Until the late 1800s, buffalo played an important role in the natural fire cycle of the prairies. The grazing herds reduced the risk of fire by pasturing the tall grasses and eliminating potential fuel for fire. However, nothing burned like dry buffalo chips, and once flames leaped into life, the wind carried smouldering chips and ashes for miles. Wherever they dropped, new fires began, feeding on mats of old, dead grass. Fertilized by ashes left in the fire's wake, new grass grew tall and lush, restarting the cycle with ideal pasture for the buffalo.

Prior to the 1870s, millions of buffalo inhabited the prairies, but by the late 1800s, the role of the buffalo in the natural fire cycle had begun to disappear because the buffalo were disappearing. Thanks to hunters and traders, they were nearing extinction. Their hides were valuable for industrial belts, winter coats, and carriage blankets; their heads were valuable to hunters and adventurers as trophies.

The best area for trading whisky for buffalo robes was the Assiniboine and Blackfoot territory of the southern prairies. Given the importance of hunting to the economy of First Nations people, guns and ammunition would have been more logical exchange items. However, traders found that alcohol was the cheapest price to pay for furs and buffalo robes. Not surprisingly, the firewater appealed to Natives, who were part of a culture that valued bravado. Firewater freed people of their inhibitions and made it easier to be fearless and brave.

The whisky trade existed in a milieu of lawlessness, rowdiness, and simple carelessness. It was this carelessness that contributed significantly to the fire hazard near whisky forts. During drunken bouts, the campfires of both Natives and traders went untended, and fighting in the vicinity sometimes caused them to spread.

The use of whisky lead to perpetual conflict on the prairies. Natives, under the influence, attacked each other and the traders they believed had cheated them. In return, the traders regarded Indians as worthless at best, except as temporary wives, cooks, and guides.

In the United States, the prejudice against the American Indian reached such proportions that policies promoting genocide became acceptable. With 3.7 million buffalo slaughtered in the early 1870s, mostly by the guns of white hunters, American Indians were starving, though not quickly enough for their detractors. As a result, the American army "endorsed a campaign to set fire to the prairies, wiping out the buffaloes' forage."[1] Once sparked on the American Great Plains, these fires wandered at will, even into Canada.

In the early 1870s, the whisky trade was very lucrative on the southwestern plains, but as the buffalo herds dwindled, unscrupulous traders looked for even cheaper ways of garnering their fortunes. Wolf pelts had gained in popularity, so traders developed a technique to get them cheaply. Known as wolfers, they poisoned buffalo carcasses with strychnine and left them on the prairies to trap wolves. The strychnine in a large bull carcass could net 120 wolf pelts.

As well as killing wolves, the poisoned carcasses also killed Indian dogs and other animals. For centuries, dogs had been essential to the nomadic people; their yelps warned of danger and kept unwanted animals from the camps. Historically, dogs were used to pull travois, move camp, and carry small children and the infirm. To Indians, therefore, the wolfers who poisoned dogs and lured other animals to ignoble deaths were even more detestable than whisky traders. Whether it was fact or fiction, Native people were said to have set fire to the poisoned carcasses and the prairie around them, deliberately driving game out of the wolfers' territories.

## *Scarlet Coats in a Scarlet Land*

The Canadian government wanted the West settled for economic and political reasons, but first, settlers needed to feel safe in the vast, lonely landscape. Canadian territorial claims also needed to be upheld.

In May 1873, the government received news of the Cypress Hills Massacre, which took place near the southern border of Saskatchewan. American whisky traders and wolfers had killed the Native men, women, and children camped there. As a result, the North-West Mounted Police (NWMP) were organized and sent into the home of the prairie fire demon to establish law and order. The first contingent made the difficult journey to Fort Dufferin; they were joined by a second contingent in mid-June. Then, on 8 July 1874, the three-hundred-member force began its long march into the West.

This epic journey of the NWMP tested even the healthiest, most fearless, and most determined of men, and their hardships became legendary. Their chosen route was a difficult one. Not only did they have inadequate food, water, transportation, and clothing throughout their journey, they also had to face the worst nature could throw at them. Rainstorms soaked them. Hail, drought, lice, mosquitoes, grasshoppers, and cold weather tormented them. Thunder and sheet lightning stampeded their horses. There were also swift rivers to cross and steep riverbanks to negotiate. And then there was fire, which would become one of their most fierce and enduring enemies.

The NWMP set out with instructions to end the whisky trade and prevent Indian wars in the West. Their specific destination was the traders' stronghold, Fort Whoop-Up, located at the present-day site of Lethbridge, Alberta. As they travelled between Fort Dufferin and the Souris River in Manitoba, the Mounties had their first inkling of what fire meant in the West. Everywhere, the prairie dust was a mixture of dirt and ashes. The men were covered with it and hated it, but there was nothing they could do about it.

The NWMP troop was spread across miles of prairie when Henri Julien, the artist accompanying them, described in his diary a fire burning at the rear of his camp:

> The spectacle was sublime. The crackling flame, the lurid light, the heavy masses of smoke rolling low at first over the surface of the grass, then mounting higher and higher, till, caught in a stratum of breeze, they veered and floated rapidly to the east, formed a scene of impressive grandeur.[2]

Although Julien himself was in no danger, teamsters still on the trail behind him were. Forced to unhook their horses from loaded carts so they could gallop out of the fire's path, they narrowly escaped disaster. Fortunately, the fickle flames left the carts and supplies untouched, but in the fire's wake was a charred landscape that posed problems for the Mounties. Soot blackened their boots and sank into their clothing. Kicked up by the men and horses in the lead, soot also flew into their faces.

The troops had other serious problems. They were strung out for miles across the prairies, and breakdowns meant individuals or small groups became stranded. When they travelled by night to catch up with the others, men sometimes lost the trail. Once lost on the prairies, they might not find their way back to the main body of men for days.

Usually flares were used to help guide men back to the trail and the rest of the troop. However, after their first experience with the ferocity of prairie fires, Commissioner French, first in command for the NWMP, was reluctant to send up flares when men were missing. The risk of fire was too great. Although others protested, he continued to wait as long as possible before ordering flares to reveal the position of the camp.

On 15 August, the troop encountered another fire burning furiously

*On 3 August 1874, artist Henri Julien painted this lightning storm, observed by the NWMP on their march west.* Glenbow Archives NA-361-9

*Since the early days of exploration in the West, artists have been fascinated with images of prairie fires. This engraving of a fire near Fort Ellice was completed in 1859 and published in* Harper's Monthly *in 1860.* Glenbow Archives NA-1406-2

near Old Wives Creek in the Saskatchewan territory. At about the same time, starvation and ill health among both the men and horses led to the force being split into three separate groups. Each was to serve and wait out the winter in a different location in the West.

On 1 October, those Mounties continuing to Fort Whoop-Up encountered yet another prairie fire that devastated a vast area. A second group, led by Colonel French, doubled back to spend the winter at Fort Pelly near Swan River. They also marched into a charred wilderness near the HBC's Fort Qu'Appelle. After five days, the contingent neared Fort Pelly where they found the barracks to be uninhabitable. Worse yet, fire had destroyed three hundred loads of hay owned by the Hudson's Bay Company, hay that had been desperately needed by the Mounties to feed their starving horses.

The third group of Mounties, under the command of Inspector Jarvis, had been ordered to Fort Ellice and then on to Fort Edmonton. Travelling with the sickest and weakest of the men and horses, the contingent faced the most physically brutal route of all, but at least they journeyed away from the fires of the southern plains as they moved northward.

During their long marches, the NWMP did not attempt to fight fires.

Their duty was to reach the whisky forts and establish law and order, but they also recorded the devastation resulting from flames racing across the West. Soon enough, their duties would include fighting the infernos.

## *Surveying Boundaries, Surveying Flames*

In 1872, the British-American Boundary Commission began surveying the forty-ninth parallel, which would define the international boundary between Canada and the United States. To mark the boundary on the prairies, surveyors built stone cairns and earth mounds, both of which were impervious to fire. At one time, survey parties were spread across 644 kilometres (400 miles) of prairie along the international boundary. Later, other boundary commissions assumed responsibility for maintaining the line, while additional survey crews established provincial boundaries and mapped the country's geography.

Early survey parties often reported prairie fires. As one of Canada's most renowned field naturalists, John Macoun went west for the first time with Sanford Fleming on an exploratory expedition in 1875. Later employed by the Geographical Surveys of Canada, he also spent 1879-1881 exploring the west. He saw many prairie fires, but the worst one occurred in October 1879. He and his assistant were working on the plains near Battleford, Saskatchewan, when they first saw long tongues of flame approaching from a distant ridge. They packed their tents and moved their horses, carts, and belongings to sandy ground where the grass was very thin. After securing their horses so they could not break away, the men waited as the fire developed into a line of flames across a nearby ridge.

The man of science, like thousands of sensitive and imaginative people over the years, described the poetic grandeur and haunting terror.

> ... with the speed of a fast horse it bore down on us. As it came near us the whirling smoke and flames seemed to take the form of living things that were in terrible agony and added largely to the sublimity of the spectacle.[3]

Macoun and his party experienced the fire's heat and smoke, but remained safe. The fire raged past them. That night, it swept into a Mounted Police camp. Although the Mounties escaped, the fire burned their tent.

Flames also destroyed the hay that had been cut by Natives of the Red Pheasant's band, 209 kilometres (130 miles) away. Unlike many of his time, Macoun did not arbitrarily blame Native people for starting countless fires.

> There is a penalty of $200 for starting a prairie fire, and as the informer gets half the fine, the Indians and Half-breeds are con-

stantly on the alert, during the dangerous season, to pounce on any delinquent. Many people blame the Indians for setting the prairie on fire, but my experience leads me to lay the blame on white men, especially the young bloods who go shooting in the fall. A stump of a cigar dropped on the prairie is much more dangerous than an Indian fire.

The fire described by Macoun was a close call for his party. Other surveyors had even closer calls. According to Samuel Anderson, he and other surveyors were working in a ravine one August day, and having watched a pillar of smoke and smelled the burning grass for days, they knew fire was nearby. However, they were uncertain of the exact path it would take.

Hard at work, the surveyors suddenly realized the fire had swept up behind them. Their camp, about 10 kilometres (6 miles) away, lay in the path of ruin. Hurrying to the camp, they tore down the tents, gathered their equipment, and threw everything into a nearby slough, their only hope of refuge from the fire.

The same August fire eventually overtook one of the commission's ox trains. For them, there was no convenient slough, so they had to create their own safe zone to survive. As the fire approached, they hurriedly burned a patch of ground, tramping out the flames as quickly as they blackened the earth. This created a dead zone, empty of fuel for the approaching fire. Once they had made the dead zone, the men drove their oxen into it. Suddenly, as the main fire closed in, the oxen panicked and ran. However, the men stayed where they were safe, and somehow, the oxen also escaped the worst of the flames.

Survey crews also started fires by accident. One labourer struck a match on his boot while standing in long grass. The grass was sparked, and the resulting fire burned a distance of 240 kilometres (150 miles). The men never learned how far south of the border the fire eventually travelled, but it was rumoured to have reached the Missouri River. At that time, Indians and Métis were being blamed for the fires that drove the few remaining buffalo as far south as the Missouri.

## Flaming Forts

The face of the southern prairies changed with the arrival of the Mounties. The first forts they built offered shelter from the elements, but little else. Still, the forts soon attracted settlers. Even former whisky traders made their homes at NWMP forts, and gradually small villages grew up around the police barracks.

Not realizing the fire danger in the West, tenderfeet accidentally started numerous fires through carelessness. Carelessness, however, was not limited to newcomers. At Fort Macleod in the Alberta territory, the foolishness of long-time resident Fred Kanouse verged on stupidity and resulted in a serious grass fire. Despite his reputation as a wild man, Kanouse knew the prairies. A former sheriff at Fort Benton, Montana, he had moonlighted as a whisky trader. After hauling kegs of alcohol to Fort Whoop-Up, he returned south of the border with his loot. There he shot a man in an argument over a horse, and suddenly he found himself on the wrong side of the American law.

The Whoop-Up range became Kanouse's refuge. At the small post that he and others built near the infamous fort, Kanouse continued bartering whisky until the arrival of the Mounties. Then, claiming to be an honest and dry trader, he opened a rooming house at Fort Macleod.

Somehow, Kanouse acquired an Indian pony suffering from mange, a disease sometimes treated by applying kerosene. So, on a hot autumn day, he doused the pony with lamp fuel and then took it to the blacksmith's shop for branding. The hot branding iron was pressed against the horse and instantly the kerosene was ablaze. The horse was doomed, and as flames caught in the prairie grass, the town was also threatened. Before the flames were extinguished, nearly a kilometre of grass had burned.

The growing village at Fort Macleod depended on the Mounties not only to fight the fires but also to provide the buckets for carrying water. By 1886, residents lamented the fire danger at meetings and in editorials. "In the whole of the town, there is not a bucket, not a ladder, no water stored, or in fact any preparation at all to fight the fiery monster."[4]

Only two water carts served the entire village's needs. According to the *Macleod Gazette*, the carts couldn't carry enough water to put out a bonfire. Besides, a trip to fill up at the river took from fifteen to twenty minutes. By then, the town could be levelled.

Pressure mounted to acquire a fire engine and waterworks. In the end, the village decided to buy fifty buckets and hire a night watchman to sound the alarm. Still, it was the Mounties who were expected to fight the fires.

On 29 October 1887, Fort Macleod again found itself in the path of a blaze. A cook's carelessness at a hunter's camp in the hills near Pincher Creek had resulted in fire. Despite strong winds, Sergeant Hetherington and his men bravely fought the fire for six hours. After successfully driving flames to the edge of the Waterton River, they assumed the fire was out. Instead, the fire smouldered throughout the following day, and by the evening of 31 October, the wind had again whipped it up to full fury.

*The first equipment used by the NWMP for fighting fire was this hand pump. It was likely a two-man pump, with each man working one handle.*
Saskatchewan Archives Board R-B2634

As flames neared Fort Macleod, all of the Mounties and townspeople fought day and night to save their town. Wagonloads of soaked blankets were pulled to a fire line that stretched for miles. Eventually, the battle against the blaze was won.

The fire had blackened a stretch of prairie 109 kilometres (68 miles) long and 24 kilometres (15 miles) wide. In the aftermath of the conflagration, blame and punishment were meted out by the local justice of the peace. Unfortunately, the $50 fine charged to the cook would never compensate for the exhaustion of the fire fighters or the destruction of precious winter pasture.

Other smaller fires broke out in Fort Macleod during the next two years, but in January 1889, the village experienced one of its worst fires yet. At 5:00 AM, the large woodpile behind the I.G. Baker store went up in flames, putting the entire town at risk.

At one time, Montana's I.G. Baker and Company had been a major supplier for the Canadian whisky trade, but after the NWMP arrived, it switched to supplying building materials and other goods to Mounties and settlers. Ironically, during the big fire of 1889, the NWMP fought hard to save the very company that had contributed to the lawlessness of the Canadian prairies by selling illegal alcohol. The I.G. Baker Company lost fifty cords of wood, but the Mounties and a few civilians saved the surrounding buildings.

That October, still another fire broke out, this time at the Fort Macleod bakery. Fortunately, police and civilians were able to confine it. Again, three years later, a dance sponsored by the NWMP at the fort was interrupted by a bugle, calling the men to a blazing store. With fire fighting all in a day's work for Mounties, the dance resumed as soon as the blaze was extinguished.

Farther east, at Fort Whoop-Up, Mounties and a former whisky trader united to fight a fiery inferno. The NWMP used several rooms in the old whisky fort as a barracks. One evening in early December 1888, some Mounties left a fire burning in the fireplace of their room while they visited another wing of the fort. Suddenly, the room burst into flames and the police cartridge belts hanging on the wall began to explode, sounding the alarm. It was already too late to save the wing from flames, and only with great difficulty were the men able to save the main building.

At one time or another, flames threatened most of the Mountie forts and the villages that sprang up around them. The NWMP were the principal fire fighters in those fires, and eventually their official job included acting as fire guardians, fire fighters, fire investigators, and lawmen with the power to lay charges against those who caused fires and those few who refused to fight fire on the prairies.

## Other Heroes and Fools

Not all fire-fighting heroes were Mounties. Many were new settlers who simply wanted to save their own land and that of their neighbours from devastation.

William Wallace and his father were settlers who had moved from Scotland to southern Manitoba to take up farming in the Canadian West. In 1882, they pitched camp near a creek that emptied into the Assiniboine River. William wrote to his sister in Scotland, describing the grandeur of the spot where they intended to build a house for the family. That same week, five men appeared at the Wallace tent, confessing they had become lost on the prairie while looking for their homestead land. The "stupid beggars quite frankly let us know that they had fired the prairie at a place where they had been smoking."[5]

By the following day, the Wallace lands were threatened by the fire. "Such an amount of flame and smoke I never before witnessed." Desperately trying to save the grassland, the only available feed for their cattle, father and son lighted small fires and beat them out to create a dead space around their tent and camp. This procedure, called backfiring, was always dangerous work. The small fires could either create a dead space wide enough to stop the oncoming fire, or if the wind was right, rage out of control and intensify the primary blaze.

William first tried to backfire near the edge of the creek, but the grass there did not light. He then went up the bank and tried again. This time

... the light started from the match like gunpowder and before we could breathe, the place was in flames. Andrew and I had terribly to run before the flames till we got up to the top of the hill where we stood, giving up all for lost.

Luckily, when the wind finally calmed, the Wallaces were able to stamp out the flames nearing their precious pasture. At one point in fighting the fire, William's boots were so hot, he thought his feet were blistering. He ignored them, however, and kept guard the rest of the night. The fire burned throughout the next day and was finally extinguished by rain.

William hated the sight of the scorched grass and burnt poplar grove and intended to have a talk with the man who started the fire. "The careless beggar ought to be informed against and fined $50, the penalty for such an action."

## Pilgrims in Distress

To William Wallace, the inferno that had threatened his land had been both magnificent and terrifying. Year after year, similar terror filled the hearts of those who moved to the prairies. Homesteads were far apart, and journeys for business, supplies, or help were long. With few people inhabiting the tiny forts and villages, there was often little assistance available for fighting the yellow and gold flames that brought distress and even death. Not surprisingly, fire became the awe-inspiring enemy of everyone living on the prairies.

As the new century approached, fur trade forts were being abandoned. The last Hudson's Bay Company fort located in the Touchwood Hills was operated by a Mr. McKenzie from 1895 to 1909. Because of his job, Mr. McKenzie was often away from the fort for days or even weeks at a time. He knew there would be little help, if any, for his wife and children if fire threatened.

One fall day, Mr. McKenzie was returning home from the Nut Lake post when he found himself in an ash shower that signalled a huge fire. With ashes falling like snowflakes, the wind whipping around him, and smoke floating over the ridge, he realized that disaster loomed for every living thing on the prairie. The dry summer and fall had turned the landscape into a tinderbox.

With his home and family on the other side of the smoke, McKenzie headed toward the fire. As the heat intensified, fire filled the horizon, and smoke blocked the sun. The wind raged, lifting flaming bunch grass into the air and dropping it, constantly creating new fires and fire lines. Flames surrounded McKenzie, and in the smoke and fire, his horses panicked. Without protection, McKenzie knew he and the horses would die. He jumped from his wagon, despite the panic in his own breast, burned a patch of ground, and pulled the team and wagon to the small island of safety.

The horses were badly spooked as the fire closed in. Knowing that both smoke and fire were deadly, McKenzie threw a blanket over their heads and crept under it with them. As flames surrounded them, the smoke was suffocating, and the heat, unbelievably intense. When the worst had passed, McKenzie pulled the blanket away, and around him, he saw a charred wilderness.

McKenzie was desperate to reach his home and family, 40 kilometres (25 miles) to the southeast, where the main fire still raged. However, he and his horses first needed water for their smoke-parched throats and he knew that somewhere nearby was a spring.

McKenzie had travelled the trail hundreds of times before, but now the land had been transformed by fire. He no longer recognized any landmarks, only the semblance of a trail. He pulled his team onto the blackened ruts, and despite his anxiety, let the recovering and parched animals walk slowly. Finally, he let them trot, but he was still confounded by the strange landscape. Unsure of where to leave the trail to find the spring, he left that decision to the horses.

Just as McKenzie was about to despair, the horses instinctively veered from the trail and picked up their pace. Other animals, some of them scorched, appeared around McKenzie and his team, all headed in the same direction. There were red foxes, badgers, and skunks—a sad-looking lot. Foxes with such badly damaged fur were called *samsons* in his trade, and McKenzie knew that not only had their fur been damaged but they had also suffered. Many would soon die, others would not live through the winter.

At the spring, the trader found other creatures that had escaped the firestorm.

The poor things did not seem at all frightened at our arrival and just watched us from a short distance. We were all pilgrims in distress. I unhitched the team but allowed them only a few mouthfuls of water and took very little myself.[6]

A natural reaction, under the circumstances, was to gulp too much water at once, resulting in bloating, in humans and animals. So McKenzie was careful, allowing himself and the horses only a little water at first. Then, once they had drunk as much as they wanted and were revived, the trader continued his journey.

On his way home, McKenzie drove through many fire lines. By sundown, the horses were exhausted and hungry. He unhitched them and rubbed them down, but there was nothing to eat. McKenzie had brought no feed and the grass was burnt. Half an hour later, with the team rested, they started out again. As McKenzie neared the post, he again saw fire, a different one than he had faced during the day.

It had come upon them from the east. The fires all around looked much worse as it began to get dark. I was about three miles from the Post and had now to go through fire all the way. I was sure from the look of things that the Post and everything else was burned ... I don't know how the horses or myself made the last mile and a half ... [*sic*]"

At last, McKenzie reached the fort. Flames had burned right up to the post, but the buildings remained standing. Inside, he found his family, exhausted but unharmed. Natives from the nearby reserve, the one remaining man at the post, and McKenzie's wife had fought furiously against the blaze.

Mrs. McKenzie was dishevelled and weary. She had gone to the reserve for help and then directed the battle against the fire near her home. After she had placed the baby in a cradle in the garden, everyone helped to pile furniture there too, for safekeeping. Finally, they beat out the flames, moving the fire back beyond the ploughed fireguard. At the fort, the threat of reemerging fire lingered for days, and flames continued to be visible on the nearby bluffs. In some places, the ground smouldered all winter.

McKenzie's wife had saved her own family from the worst prairie fire they would ever know, but others hadn't been so lucky. In some areas, people had died in the flames, and hundreds of wild animals and livestock had also lost their lives.

## The Sacred Hill

One story concerning prairie fire at the turn of the century is told within the Native oral tradition by Fred Yellow Old Woman, the grandson of Deerfoot, a renowned Blackfoot runner. He tells of a hill—a sacred place of vision quests—not far to the south and east of present-day Calgary. Its Blackfoot name, given as the result of a prairie fire, tells its history.

As a young boy, Yellow Old Woman did not know the hill's history. He visited it many times with his parents and elders. Young, smart, and a little arrogant, he became impatient when the elders gave offerings and said prayers. "Why do you do this?" he finally asked, and the elders told him about the fire at the sacred hill.

Everything, including the hill, had its place in their lives. From a distance, it seemed like only a small rise, but the hill was as high as other important landmarks of the Blackfoot. Still, it was not its height that had made it sacred. It had become a place of prayer and offerings because it had been the scene of great loss.

Near the turn of the century, a tribe had been travelling across open prairie when a wildfire, started by lightning, raged toward them. As quickly as possible, they sought refuge at a nearby hill. There, they offered hurried prayers. Then, at the base of the hill, the people set small fires to create a space where the wildfire could not cross. At the top of the hill, they dug holes so some might jump into them and be protected from the flames. Women, children, and elders gathered to wait and watch high on the hill. Below and around them, fire raged.

Young braves circled the base of the hill. They battled fiercely against the flames. Fighting to keep the others safe, they sacrificed their lives. Yet the fire was so fierce and hot, it could not be stopped. Before all danger passed, a third of the tribe had died. It was only then that the hill was named *Itsiboksikasoyi*, The Place Where the People Burned Their Feet.

Whether the hill, a high point on the open plain, had provided refuge for just one fire, or for many, is unknown. However, as a scene of great tragedy and sacrifice, it has occupied a sacred place in the Blackfoot tradition for generations.[7]

# CHAPTER THREE

# A Range Ablaze
# 1880-1900

With law and order established in the West, ranchers and farmers saw a future for themselves on the southern prairies. They did not foresee the problem of fire. Many blamed fires on CPR locomotives spewing steam, smoke, and sparks across the plains, and some demanded financial compensation. While legal and political wrangling took place over the issue, farmers and ranchers fought fires, suffering enormous losses in livestock and property. At the same time, stories about fires, heroic fire-fighting efforts, and culprits began to circulate.

## Pastures of Plenty

For ranchers, the wide-open prairie was the land of their dreams. The Districts of Alberta and Assiniboia (site of present-day Saskatchewan) were particularly suited for grazing livestock, and grazing leases were available from the government for next to nothing. Native grasslands, where the buffalo had roamed, offered ample summer feed for livestock in good years. However, ranchers soon learned that adequate pasture was at a premium in drought-stricken summers, and everything they owned could go up in smoke.

Every year from early spring to late fall, huge tracts of land were charred, especially in the Palliser Triangle. In August 1881, after riding from Fort Walsh to Fort Macleod, Mountie W.H. Cox reported the fire devastation of a 129-kilometre (80-mile) strip of land. Whether it had been sparked by a campfire, a carelessly dropped match, or lightning, the fire had painted the landscape black.

In October 1883, one pioneer Saskatchewan farmer lost oats, stable,

The first organized fire-fighting efforts consisted of volunteer bucket brigades; many men also volunteered the services of their horses. Both men and horses earned a small fee for their services. Early fire departments usually kept extra buckets, axes, and water barrels on hand. City of Lethbridge Archives and Records Management P19739518000

harness, horse blankets, and more than 71 tonnes (70 tons) of hay to fire. The grass had been long, and the fire had flared during a tremendous wind.

We had first class fire breaks but they were no use, as the fire blew for hundreds of yards ahead. A chunk of lighted grass carried by the wind lit on one of the oat stacks, and then the fire spread to the other stacks. It was a whirlwind, travelling about fifty miles an hour, and the piece that set fire to the stack lit near the top where the stack was drawn in. It was a dry fall; everything was quite dry; we saved the wheat which was stacked a little farther north from the oats; we had hard fighting but we saved it.[1]

No season was ever free from the threat of fire. Mild winters in the Chinook belt meant livestock could pasture much of the season. However, when there was little snow cover, the fire hazard skyrocketed.

Ranchers and farmers depended on the NWMP to ride fire patrol, organize the fire-fighting effort, and battle the flames. According to Inspector Samuel Steele, who rode west in 1874 and served in the force for forty years, the moment the police saw smoke or fire, one Mountie would ride to the hot spot.

[Others] in the party had to turn out every male settler, man or boy, within ten miles to extinguish it. Waggons loaded with barrels of water and empty sacks were soon going at full speed to the fire; mounted men with damp sacks tied to their saddles rode furiously in that direction; ploughs were brought to run lines of fire guards to cut off the area in flames. When the grass was short the fires were extinguished by beating out the flames with wet sacks. Sometimes I had a hundred men out for several days at a time; everything was set aside for this. All the officers and men of my two divisions were fire guardians under the law of the territory.[sic][2]

At the height of fire season, barrels of water, gunnysacks, and old brooms were kept ready in wagons, and horses were kept harnessed. Still, fighting fires was both backbreaking and heartbreaking work.

Each year, there seemed to be more fires, and many wondered why. In the minds of ranchers, settlers, and police, the new railway was the culprit, and something had to be done about it.

## Canadian Pacific Railway—Trail of Fire

From the time the Canadian Pacific Railway (CPR) began its journey across the West, the company was plagued by fire. Grassland fires were blamed on sparks from steam locomotives and on ashes dumped from trains. Fires also

*These two steam locomotives belched clouds of smoke as they crossed the prairies. Visible alongside the track is a small burn area. Embers and hot ashes from trains likely started this fire and many others like it.* Provincial Archives of Alberta A-5206

created havoc for the railway by destroying offices, stations, sheds, and freight.

In October 1882, fire ravaged the building that housed the office of railway champion William Cornelius Van Horne. Firemen, who had just extinguished flames in another building, reacted immediately and sprayed 105,991 litres (28,000 gallons) of water on the fire. In the end, the building was saved, but Van Horne lost everything in his office.

The loss of office space due to fire was nothing compared to the nightmare prairie fires created for Van Horne. The ranchers and farmers who owned land beside the railway tracks suffered most from the infernos. To them, the CPR was a mammoth enemy, but other small railway companies were also held responsible for starting fires. Almost as soon as railway tracks were in place, ranchers and farmers began waging a battle with the railways that would last for decades.

One of the most fervent warriors in the battle against the railways was a retired army officer, Major General T. Strange. He was president of the Military Colonization Ranche Company near Gleichen, Alberta. Like other ranchers and newly arrived homesteaders, Strange quickly learned the fickle nature of life in the West. One day, pasture might be plentiful and crops bountiful. Only days later, the same area might be reduced to wasteland by fire. In fact, just after the arrival of the railway, Strange's ranch lost its entire pasturage to fire.

To Strange, the loss of feed was no trivial matter, for the ranch had seven hundred cattle and three hundred horses. Not only did he have to find feed and pasture for his livestock after the fire but he also had the time-consuming work of moving the livestock to another district.

The Major General was prepared to take on the culprit responsible for his losses, and according to Strange, that culprit was the Canadian Pacific Railway. Belching smoke and sparks, steam locomotives left a trail of fire in their wake, and the Military Colonization Ranche was due its damages. When the railway denied responsibility, Strange wrote to the prime minister and filed a lawsuit against the CPR.

Van Horne thought Strange was a crackpot. Nevertheless, he launched an investigation. The CPR investigators concluded that campfires and similar accidents caused some prairie fires. However, they felt most were set by buffalo bone hunters, who fired the long grass so that the white bones would be more visible on the blackened landscape.

*During the summer of 1888, James Sanderson and his Métis crew collected this pile of buffalo bones near Medicine Hat to sell for use in fertilizer, explosives, and bleach. Some blamed Métis crews for firing the prairie to see the bones more clearly against the blackened land.* Medicine Hat Museum and Art Gallery PC62.9

Strange lost his legal battle, but he was not prepared to concede defeat. On 13 November 1885, a prairie fire spread from Milk River Ridge to the Lethbridge area, and every able-bodied person had been needed to fight it. When the governor general visited Alberta shortly thereafter, Strange toured him through the devastated landscape. He also expressed his wish that, near ranches and towns, the CPR should be required to plough six furrows along the tracks, to act as fireguards. The Queen's representative took Strange's message back to Ottawa.

For Strange, that was still not enough. Together with other ranchers, he organized the Canadian Northwest Territories Stock Association. By 1886, the stockmen were actively pressuring the CPR for cooperation. The association also passed its own fire-related rules. When fire struck, all members within 24 kilometres (15 miles) of the fire were to inform their nearest neighbours of the calamity. Then they were to help battle the blaze. The fine for not complying was $50, at a time when a quality, two-seater wagon could be purchased for about $30.

Two years later, the association petitioned the Canadian government, demanding fireguards be ploughed on both sides of the tracks. In addition, it requested that the debris and grass between the guards be burned off each fall.

## 1889—Mounties and Firestorms

Firestorms pose a serious threat on the prairies. They are generated by fires so hot and intense that they suck air from the surroundings, creating their own violent wind currents. Ash from firestorms can rain down on land miles away from the original source.

According to NWMP reports, 1889 was one of the worst firestorm years on the prairies. The year began with little snow cover and spring melts arrived earlier than usual. The weather was warm, dry, and windy. Still, for many Westerners, the weather seemed ideal. In fact, it was perfect—for fires.

Firestorms attacked nearly every district patrolled by the Mounties that year. Usually, the southern prairies were devastated by fire more frequently than the central and northern areas of the provinces. However, in 1889, the risk was high throughout the western territories. From February to May 1889, flames raged everywhere. On one occasion, all residents and policemen in the Fort Macleod district were needed to fight ten large fires and several small ones.

On 4 April 1889, Superintendent Richard Burton Deane, a member of the first NWMP troop to arrive in the West, was called to help fight a fire,

*Prairie Fire – the Only Enemy the Mounted Failed to Face.* Compliments
RCMP Retired Veterans Association, Scarlet & Gold, 1922, Glenbow Archives

reportedly about 19 to 24 kilometres (12 to 15 miles) away. He and nine
other Mounties set out, well equipped with supplies. However, fires played
tricks on the plains and locating the front line of a fire could be difficult.
Deane wrote:

> We had first to find a ford across the Belly River, then to climb the
> opposite bank upon a road of our own making, and next we headed
> straight for the centre of the fire. We left barracks at eight o'clock in

the evening, and travelled until three o'clock next morning. We seemed then to be just as far from the fire as when we started, but were fortunate enough to find some water, so we halted for an hour to rest and feed the horses.[sic][3]

Short on rations, Deane decided to turn back. He and his men did not reach the barracks until noon, and by then they had travelled over 80 kilometres (50 miles).

Again, two days later, the fire appeared to be about 12 kilometres (8 miles) away. Deane and his men left the barracks at 9:00 PM and rode 24 kilometres (15 miles) before reaching the fire. By 5:30 AM the next day, they had extinguished the last flames and returned to the barracks.

Puzzled by the discrepancies in distance, they eventually realized that the fire had burned in an arc. On their first time out, they had ridden toward the centre of the arc, the point farthest from their barracks. This had not been obvious on the smoke-filled horizon.

Fires also flared that fall. On 17 September, a NWMP party left Fort Macleod to extinguish a blaze on the Cochrane range. On 18 September, two more parties were needed for a blaze in the south. Then, on 19 September, a civilian named Macklin was arrested for setting one of the two fires and was fined $100 or three months in jail. Again, on 25 September, more men were called out for a fire to the south. Not until 26 September did life at the fort return to normal.[4]

For the division stationed at Maple Creek, in what is now Saskatchewan, fighting fires that spring and fall seemed endless and futile work. Police and area residents would put out a fire in one area only to find another had sprung up elsewhere. The air filled with smoke, winds were strong, and flames flickered day and night. Settlers lost farms, feed, and pasture. Some fires burned for two weeks.

In Saskatchewan, the worst fire of 1889 had begun between the Sweet Grass and Cypress Hills. Burning a swath eastward, it reduced old Fort Walsh to soot and rubble. Settlers in the Regina area lost supplies, and their fields were laid waste. In the fertile belt to the north, grass and forest fires blended into single infernos at times.

In March, the Battleford district fell victim to fire. Prince Albert and Saskatoon were also endangered, and in Alberta, Fort Saskatchewan was hit by flames. The Calgary, Sheep Creek, St. Mary's River, and Lethbridge areas were also blackened by fire. With sloughs and small lakes dried up, and few natural fire barriers on the prairies, the hazard continued until fall.

## The Dead Zones

One of the fires of 1889 raged toward a CPR camp near Craven, Saskatchewan, where construction engineer P. Turner Bone was in charge. A teamster pulled into camp one day and shouted warnings of a fire being carried by fierce wind. Realizing they would be unable to stop the fire, the men immediately began the risky business of creating a safety zone. They started small fires and quickly extinguished them, until they had blackened an area large enough to hold themselves, their camp supplies, and equipment. As the conflagration neared, the men were seared by the tremendous heat that preceded it, but the dead land of the safety zone offered no fuel for the fire, thus saving men and equipment.

There were also other kinds of dead zones—those created by the prairie fire demon itself—and the 76 Ranch near Swift Current, Saskatchewan, was one of the victims. Sir John Lister-Kaye, an English-born baronet, had bought more than ten sections of land, east of Regina, from the government and the CPR. He scouted and purchased other huge tracts of land, with the intention of having ten ranches in all; seven of these would lie between Swift Current and Calgary, which was the worst part of the semiarid fire belt. To Lister-Kaye, proximity to the CPR tracks was an advantage for shipping livestock and grain. It was also a disadvantage in terms of fire hazard.

By 1889, each of his ranches was stocked with about 65 horses, 500 cows, 2000 sheep, and 90 hogs. The future looked promising, and sheds were built to house 5000 sheep and 300 hogs. Then in 1890, winter weather became an enemy. The snow was too deep for livestock to forage, and without adequate feed, Lister-Kaye's livestock losses were enormous. Still, he remained optimistic; the deep snow had melted earlier than usual.

That spring, the ranch had 2200 sheep grazing near Gull Lake, Saskatchewan, and most of the ewes were to give birth. Then, on 16 April, sparks from a CPR locomotive set the nearby prairie ablaze. Still wrapped in their heavy winter fleeces, the sheep were quickly trapped by the fire. Before the flock could be moved to safety and the fire extinguished, the fleece of hundreds of the poor animals caught fire. More than half the sheep died or were so badly injured they had to be put down by demoralized ranch hands.

That summer brought drought to the ranch, with obvious consequences. Unfortunately, Lister-Kaye lost the confidence of his investors and was pressured into resigning. Yet, even in the years to come, the change in management would not protect the huge ranching syndicate from suffering additional devastation from raging fire demons.

The approach of the fire demon was terrifying to everyone, but especially to women whose children were in the paths of flames. Eliza May was one such woman. Ernest May, one of Calgary's first photographers, had immigrated to the area in 1886. During the next two years, May set himself up and prepared a home for his bride-to-be. Eliza arrived from England in 1888. They were married and a year later they had a son.

By October 1889, Ernest had built a small ranch house at a beautiful spot on the Elbow River, in sight of the Rocky Mountains. The couple moved into their home in November. The next summer, Ernest put up hay on shares with a man who owned land west of Brushy Ridge, about 24 kilometres (15 miles) from the Mays.

Early in March 1891, Ernest rode out to fight a fire after seeing smoke off to the west, in the vicinity of his hay fields. With the baby to care for and her husband away, Eliza did not sleep that first night. Instead, she watched the progress of the smoke. By early morning, flames had reached a plateau close to their home.

The noise of the roar of the flames was so great that it sounded like hundreds of wagons rattling along. About 8:00 AM it was within a

*Volunteers battling grassfires usually used wet sacks to beat out flames; the constant bending was backbreaking, so they often tied their wet sacks to broom handles.* Glenbow Archives NA-1502-1

mile of our house but was separated from it by a small watering place. I was just preparing to go down to the creek with our little son and a few treasures in the baby carriage when I saw Harry Gray, coming to see if he could help in any way. I was very glad to have somebody close at hand in case of need. We tied sacks to long sticks and soaked them in water all ready to begin our turn of fighting fire if need be, the wind changed a bit and the fire burst all over the plateau towards Calgary.[5]

The following year, the Circle Ranch, near Gleichen, Alberta, fell victim to fire. The ranch's cowboys fought the demon with wet sacks and brooms, but the dead zone created by the fire was constantly expanding, and every living thing in the demon's path was in danger. Flames in short grass country did not always leap high into the air. Instead, they licked at prairie wool, the drought-resistant blue gama grass prevalent on the prairies. Growing close to the ground, the native grass fuelled fires that travelled at unbelievable speeds.

In the sparsely populated prairies, there were simply not enough people to spread across the fire line to beat out flames. Horses could gallop along the line faster than men could run it, and that extra speed made a difference in fighting the infernos. Out of necessity, ranchers determined a means of using what was at hand—horses and the carcasses of slaughtered livestock—to attack the fire demon.

On the Circle Ranch, fourteen cattle were quickly slaughtered. Carcasses were cut in half, and cowboys rode along the fire line dragging the damp carcasses to wet and smother the flames. Amazingly, the well-trained horses obeyed their riders, despite their instinctual terror of fire. They galloped as close to the fire line as possible. Flames licked at them, and twenty-eight of the valued horses suffered burns to their hooves and shins. Following behind the horse-drawn carcasses, men beat out embers that smouldered in the grass roots. The fire fighters had to be thorough because winds could fan embers back to life, with disastrous consequences.

# CHAPTER FOUR

# *Wooden Towns*

During the last two decades of the nineteenth century, few years passed without the fire monster roaring across the range. The impact of fire in prairie towns was equally devastating. In fact, town fires and range fires were not necessarily separate events. A fire might begin in town and be carried to open spaces, or it might begin in the open and race toward town. Burning unchecked and carried by the wind, it could threaten every resident and building of the new towns and villages. There, although more people were in immediate danger than before, more hands were also available to battle the blazes.

*Belongings piled in the street were a common sight when fire roared through the buildings of early towns. Townspeople saved what they could and watched as buildings were levelled. This fire raged in Outlook, Saskatchewan.* Glenbow Archives NA-2642-60

## *Threatened Communities*

Fire in the fields and wild lands of the West displayed many changing and frightening moods. In prairie communities, the lurking enemy displayed just as many transformations. However, in towns it also had the potential to devastate large numbers of people in a single attack.

Early citizens witnessed the devastation wrought by fire again and again. They watched fire destroy the homes and businesses of neighbours and friends, and lived with a constant, nagging fear. For some, fear of fire was seldom far from their thoughts, and for others, fear often escalated to anxiety.

Logically, prairie towns faced a much higher risk from fire than coastal towns or interior towns in other parts of Canada. In the earliest of prairie villages, those of the Native people and Métis, fire could wreak havoc. An example of this occurred at the Métis village at Wood Mountain, a boundary post for the NWMP in what now is Saskatchewan. By the 1870s, the Métis from Cypress Mountain had moved to Wood Mountain. Father Hugonard also brought his flock of French families from Qu'Appelle to the bustling community. Then, disaster struck when a huge prairie fire swept through the village. The destruction forced the Métis and French families to move to the nearby district of Willow Bunch, where game was more plentiful.

*During the autumn of 1879, a fire blackened the landscape near this NWMP post at Wood Mountain, Saskatchewan. Forage for wildlife disappeared as did the wildlife itself, and the next spring, local Indians were starving. As a result, about thirty Métis families were forced to move to more plentiful hunting grounds.* Glenbow Archives NA-2003-49

When the newly arrived settlers first built their towns, many did not realize they were building in the land of the fire demon. However, they learned soon enough of the semiarid conditions, the strong winds, and the phenomenal lightning storms. They learned that fire could light upon them from the plains, and that fire could also be carried from the villages out to the open spaces. Still, life without fire seemed impossible. Life without stoves, forges, and lamps was life without amenities, and the villages and towns were trying to provide as many amenities as possible to the new settlers stepping down from each wagon and train.

The enormous influx of people to prairie villages and towns happened over a very brief time span. Many communities began as NWMP posts, missions, or railway divisional points. Soon, a tent town would be established, then log shacks appeared, and later, dozens of wooden buildings were constructed, giving a greater sense of permanency to the recent arrivals. Yet, all of these early building materials were ready fuel for hungry flames.

During the settlement years, the fire season in towns coincided to some extent with the fire season for the vast landscape beyond the last streets. The tinder dry conditions and winds were the same in villages as elsewhere on the prairie, but the potential for accidents grew with the arrival of each new person. In towns, as well as on homesteads, danger lay waiting inside kerosene lamps during long, dark winter nights. Ill-fitting stovepipes and defective chimneys also contributed to conflagrations. Some businesses, such as blacksmith shops and livery stables, were at greater risk for fire than others. There were hundreds of ways uncontrolled fires might start.

Despite the large numbers of townspeople threatened by fire, fighting the flames during freezing weather was often impossible. Ice covered the lakes and rivers, the only source of water. Few towns had adequate waterworks, and fire-fighting equipment was often minimal. What would begin as a small fire could race out of control, destroying an entire town. Not surprisingly, fire often changed the face of a prairie village, town, or city forever.

## Winnipeg—Gateway City Ablaze

For thousands of fur traders and settlers, Winnipeg was the last major shopping centre on their journeys west or north. It was a commercial hub for the railways and a freight yard full of goods waiting to be shipped. As such, Winnipeg would experience more fires than many other quiet, more stable communities. Small fires took their toll in the city's early days, but the devastating fires of the 1880s and 1890s meant the city was in a continual state of building and rebuilding. Although terrified people escaped with their lives, block after block of buildings were reduced to ashes. Damage from individual fires in Winnipeg during later years would be even more devastating.

For the thousands who chose to make Winnipeg their home, lumber was, for the most part, the building material of the day. Countless cords of wood, awaiting use in the construction of houses, businesses, and sidewalks, made perfect fuel for fire. The same held true for piles of freight, much of it destined for farther west. Kerosene, dynamite, and gunpowder were especially explosive and combustible. Sidewalks and floors, which were oiled to keep down the dust, also added fuel to fire.

When it came to fire, however, the greatest uncontrollable factor would always be weather. Wind and fire were mighty allies, and their relationship became the source of deep-seated fear in western families. When frigid temperatures and inadequate or inoperable equipment were added to the equation, communities were often paralyzed in the battle against fire.

Although Winnipeg would not be razed by a single conflagration, one fire after another meant the face of the young community was constantly changing.[1] Many areas of the city were built, burned down, and built again.

In December 1882, Winnipeg firemen tackled one of the many fires that plagued them that winter. The cause was a common one at the time: an oil lamp had either tipped over or burst. During the response, a fire engine pump froze, a hose ruptured, and the water supply was inadequate. The circumstances resulted in the first death in a Winnipeg fire; the victim was a man too ill to make a timely escape.

Six months later, in another fire, a fortunate rescue was made by a hotel proprietor who wrapped himself in a blanket to save the child of a hotel guest. However, a faulty water hydrant complicated fire fighting, and the fire took its toll by gutting twelve buildings.

Nineteen buildings went up in smoke in the Princess Opera House fire of 1892. Then, two years later, on 16 November 1894, Winnipeg was assaulted by one of the worst fires ever. A fire threatened the Western Canada Building on the corner of Portage and Main Streets in downtown Winnipeg, an area that would often succumb to flames. The alarm for this fire was raised at 2:00 AM. An alarm was raised for a second fire at 4:30 AM, before the first fire was under control—the Grand Union hotel was on fire. The desk clerk and a cabby immediately pounded on doors to rouse hotel guests, but it took the fire department thirty minutes to organize their response to the hotel fire. One of their engines had broken down, and one of their pumpers was in disrepair. As the wind was whipped into gale-force proportions, the hotel became a raging inferno. Fire spread rapidly, engaging about a dozen businesses and homes in all.

Desperately in need of another pumper, Winnipeg telegraphed Portage la Prairie for help. The CPR was prepared to run a special train to bring the equipment to the hotel fire, but surprisingly, Winnipeg's neighbour stalled. What if a fire threatened Portage la Prairie before the pumper could be returned? The authorities finally decided to send the pumper, but the decision came too late to help Winnipeg. The fire had already subsided, and the equipment was no longer needed.

In February, four years later, wind was again a factor when the first McIntyre Block, at the time the city's most impressive business building, was razed. The fire began at 7:00 AM; walls were crumbling by 1:00 PM. Fifty offices, three association halls, the offices of the University of Manitoba, and the university's Isbister Library were all lost.

In February 1899, fire destroyed the Northern Pacific and Manitoba Railway hotel, another of the city's finest buildings. The fire had started in a fourth-floor fireplace. Temperatures had plummeted, and hose lines froze in the bitter cold. Two pumps broke, and the water pressure was insufficient to fight the blaze. Although bricks had been used to build many of Winnipeg's important buildings, including the hotel, the intensity of the heat crumbled the masonry and the building was destroyed. The adjoining railway offices, depot, and freight sheds also fell victim to the blaze. Fortunately, no lives were lost.

On 11 October 1904, the night watchman of the newly remodelled Bullman Block walked into a cloud of smoke as he began his nightly rounds of the building's basement. The elevator acted like a chimney flue, and the building was fully enveloped in flame before firemen from the station across the street could tackle the blaze. A strong wind spread the fire to a hotel and several other business blocks; city hall and the newspaper office were threatened. Dozens of spectators, fascinated by the power and terror of fire, stood by.

The embers that touched down on the Ashdown Hardware posed a new danger. Inside the store were everyday supplies, including explosives such as kerosene, paint, and gun powder. Despite the danger, spectators ignored fire fighters' pleas to move to safety. Suddenly, however, the sharp crack of rifle shells and other exploding ammunition emphasized the hazard, and the spectators fled.

Eight years later, in 1912, Winnipeg fell victim to the unthinkable, the

*Four firemen died fighting the Winnipeg Theatre fire of 23 December 1926. Fighting winter fires was enormously difficult because hoses and engines often froze and became inoperable.* Provincial Archives of Manitoba

torch of an arsonist, and the facts were as fascinating as any fiction. In the meantime, thousands of settlers flowed through Winnipeg, moving farther west and north. In new prairie towns and cities, crowded conditions and quickly constructed buildings created fire risk, as did inadequate water supplies and fire-fighting equipment, wind, and frigid temperatures. In the new communities farther west, some of these problems were even more extreme than in Winnipeg.

## Qu'Appelle and the CPR

The NWMP fort of Qu'Appelle was built by Major Walsh as a police barracks on the fur trade route. However, with the coming of the railway in the spring of 1882, a boom began, and by fall of that year, the CPR had built an Immigration Hall to accommodate new settlers.

The hall stood next to the railway sheds and yards, where the CPR stored goods to be shipped farther west. In places, coal oil soaked the ground. Kegs of gunpowder, dynamite, and other explosives used for hunting, railway building, and coal mining were safely stored in the sheds before being loaded on the trains. Then, in May 1893, someone carelessly dropped a match in front of CPR freight sheds. Not surprisingly, the oil-soaked ground began to burn.[2]

As the fire spread, one of the buildings filled with dynamite fell victim to the flames. It exploded and burning fragments fell on the roof of the Immigration Hall. The sight was terrifying as flames destroyed the hall and spread from there to the post office, the billiard hall, and five stores. A bucket brigade managed to save the hotel, but for the most part, the fire just burned itself out. The town had been devastated.

At a meeting with the CPR that night, people were distraught. They criticized the railway for storing explosives so close to human habitation, and for not having proper fire-fighting equipment. For too long, the CPR had ignored the pleas of the people, angry residents claimed. When the Immigration Hall was being built, many of them had protested its location so close to CPR yards. What's more, they pointed out that perhaps the fire could have been stopped if there had been open space around the yards.

The complaints did not end with that meeting. The editorial writer for the *Winnipeg Free Press* noted that the least the CPR could do was bring in lumber, free of charge, for a new Immigration Hall, which would cost $10,000 to rebuild. By 1884, the CPR had provided the cheap lumber. In addition, the community had organized a volunteer fire brigade. However, some of the promise shown by Qu'Appelle in its earliest days had been lost.

## *Lucky Regina*

For a prairie town in the fire belt, Regina was fortunate. Trained help in case of fire was available from the Mountie post nearby, and fate seemed to smile on the community. However, Regina was not without its risks. Water was at a premium, and Regina's location on the wide open plains meant winds could create havoc. Eventually, the community was to suffer the most serious devastation of any prairie city, but in the early days, the only ruin was caused by wind. Had wind and fire ever joined forces, the community would have been wiped from the map.

Early residents of Regina knew that the police stationed at the edge of town would help fight fires, but in the 1880s, volunteer fire fighters also met regularly to practise. At the time, men not only volunteered their services but they also volunteered their teams of horses. Men and horses were willing, but fire-fighting equipment was minimal, and there was no local support for buying more. The volunteers once had to fight a fire at the Anglican Bishop's house with wet blankets, and as late as 1886, they only had a hand pumper to use.

On 15 March 1890, during the first large fire in Regina, fire-fighting equipment was still primitive, but volunteers and eighty Mounties battled

On 4 September 1905, this Regina Fire Brigade still relied on volunteer horses. The following year, the community purchased its first horse team for the fire department—Percherons, Dick and Jerry. By 1939, Regina fire horses had all been retired in favour of motorized vehicles. Some of the retired horses were transferred to garbage detail; accustomed to racing to fires, they galloped along their routes, spilling garbage. City of Regina Archives F-17

Crowds gathered to observe the spectacular fire at the grandstand on the Regina exhibition grounds in 1917. City of Regina Archives RPL-B-523

the blaze. It was windy, and after three hours, the tinder-dry buildings along an entire block had succumbed, though no one died.

Another bad fire burned in 1892. Twice, the town council proposed that money be allotted for fire-fighting equipment, but both times the initiative was turned down by taxpayers. However, the waterworks had been extended by 1906, and finally, a central fire hall was erected. In 1912, firemen were also given a red-and-white chemical fire engine, and a hose truck with a bell and horn.

On 30 June 1912, Regina was visited both by terrible devastation and a modicum of good luck. The cyclone that ripped through the city crumpled buildings, including the local grain elevator. Thousands were left homeless and twenty-eight were found dead, but thankfully, the community didn't burn. Had fire taken hold, there would have been nothing left but a blackened landscape. The rain that followed the cyclone may have seemed an added curse when there was so much to do, but in the land of the fire demon, it was really a blessing.

In 1913, the volunteer fire fighters disbanded. They had responded to 148 fire alarms that year, and their work had become demanding enough to necessitate full-time paid firemen.[3] With the change, the city made better preparations for the fires of the future, and by 1938, the department was entirely mechanized.

## Calgary—The Sandstone City

Cowtown began its transformation into the Sandstone City in response to fires and fire danger. In 1883, George Murdock, who later become mayor of Calgary, recognized the problem of fire near the community. In his diary entry for 9 July, he noted the woods at Shaganappi were on fire. The next day he wrote that smoke was so thick in places, he could barely see any distance.

From its earliest days, Calgary had little in the way of fire protection. It suffered both from water and weather problems. Like other prairie towns, the community could not afford adequate water works for fighting fires. For instance, in January of 1885, people resorted to throwing snowballs to douse a house fire.

That spring, Mayor Murdock suggested wells should be drilled to fulfil the community's water needs. Cribbing the wells would cost $1.50 per foot, nails would cost $15, and a platform for each well would be $8.50. Assuming the wells would be drilled 8 metres (25 feet) deep, the basic cost per well would be about $60.[4] Additional costs would bring the total to $87 per well.

The project was expensive, but the town council decided to take out a loan and sink nine wells. The entire process would take about three months.

By late August 1885, Calgary had organized its first fire brigade, with a captain, two hookmen, two axemen, and two ladder men, one of whom was the well-known Cappy Smart. The volunteer firemen, each paid seventy-five cents per blaze, claimed to have perfect attendance at fires. However, others also helped.

The community also decided to purchase a chemical engine and hook and ladder equipment from Winnipeg. When the new equipment finally arrived, Calgary still hadn't raised the money to pay for it, so the manufacturer had custom officials keep it locked away until payment could be made.

All the right plans were in place on the Sunday morning when disaster struck. At 2:00 AM on 15 October 1886, the centre of town caught fire. There was a terrible southwest wind, and the bucket brigade worked furiously to save several wooden buildings that were already in flames. However, by the time the fire department arrived, fire threatened the entire town. Always uncontrollable and often merciless, the wind had shifted, spreading flames to the north.

Calgarians were desperate to save their town; they knew they needed the new fire engine, even if it hadn't yet been properly purchased. People fighting the fire headed for the customs house. Quickly, volunteer firemen and law-abiding citizens smashed down the door of the shed where the fire engine was being stored. They dragged out the engine, and in short order, it was doing the job it had been designed to do. It took over a day to be sure the fire was out, and fourteen buildings were destroyed,[5] but the rest of Cowtown was saved from becoming puffs of smoke on the plains.

Nonetheless, damage to the city was extensive, and some volunteers resigned from the new fire department because so little equipment was available for fighting flames. Eventually, a new brigade was formed, one in which the well-paid fire chief, mayor, councillors, and fire fighters were supposed to deal with fire issues. When it became apparent the new system was also flawed with too many decision makers, citizens wanted the old brigade reinstated once again. Fire politics continued to be heated in the community for a long time, with interesting results.

Soon, Calgary fire fighters were tackling fires with 610 metres (2000 feet) of hose, the Ronald Fire Engine, and two hand-drawn fire reels. Despite the presence of newly drilled wells and two rivers, having water in the right place at the right time was a problem, so the progressive community looked elsewhere to minimize the fire hazard.

*Captain Cappy Smart, at the right edge of the photo, directed Calgary firemen in this winter fire.* Glenbow Archives NB-16-429

*This fire in downtown Calgary, on 7 November 1886, changed the face of the community forever.* Glenbow Archives NA-298-3

One solution lay underground. Calgary had been established near vast quantities of sandstone, a building material the fire demon could not devour. After the great fire of 1886, sandstone became the construction product of choice in Calgary, for those who could afford it.

The first sandstone quarry near Calgary opened in 1886, and others soon followed. By the 1890s, fifty percent of Calgary's tradesmen were stone masons working with sandstone. The first new sandstone building was the Knox Presbyterian Church, completed in 1887. By 1888, the new courthouse and other sandstone buildings were giving the community a new face.

As the new saviours of the fire-wracked community, stone masons were well paid, often earning $2 a day, which was twice the wage of general construction workers. Work was plentiful, and many stone masons worked ten-hour days, six-and-a-half days a week.

Eventually, the choice of building with sandstone was related as much to the town's preferred image of itself as it was to fire prevention and safety. Sandstone was substantial, permanent, and even dignified according to many of the community's businesspeople. These were the qualities they wanted for their homes, as well as their businesses. The building boom continued, and for years, sandstone sales soared.

The new Sandstone City had a much more sophisticated image than the old Cowtown. During this period, fire fighting became the job of professionals. As a result, frame houses and stores were still considered safe enough for ordinary people. Nevertheless, fire had permanently changed the face of the Calgary community, just as it had affected hundreds of other wooden towns on the prairies.

# Methods and Madness

During the early decades of the twentieth century, the fire fiend crossed the prairies at will. Named the Destroyer by some, fire seemed unconquerable. Those fighting fire soon learned their best chance for winning was being organized and methodical. Fire guardians became watchdogs with special responsibilities for organizing fire-fighting efforts. Individuals and communities created fireguards, strips of fallow land too wide for fires to jump. Farmers and ranchers challenged the railroads. Fire departments, equipment, and insurance grew in importance, but still, people's greatest ally was dogged persistence. Unfortunately, they faced an enemy of equally strong will.

## The Insane Years

From 1901 to 1904, the entire Palliser Triangle seemed to be in flames at one time or another. In the *Annual Report of the North-West Mounted Police Force for the Year 1901*, the police commissioner suggested that a fire near Gleichen had likely been more destructive than any other in the history of the West. That year, fires spread along the border for hundreds of miles, from east to west and as far as a hundred miles to the north.

In 1902, as ranches made way for farms and settlements, billowing clouds of black smoke filled the Maple Creek and Piapot Creek districts of Saskatchewan. Only one of many blazes at the time, this fire travelled 16 kilometres (10 miles) distance and was as much as 16 kilometres (10 miles) wide in places. At first, twenty men fought the fire, but they were soon joined by twenty more. All day and night they ploughed fireguards, beat at the blaze, and smothered flames with green cowhides. However, in

*The smoke from burning grain stooks in this Saskatchewan field greatly reduced visibility in the area.* Saskatchewan Archives Board R-B7495-21

the end it was a wind shift and rain that brought victory over the foe.

The fall of 1903 was hot and dry, and southern Alberta suffered badly from fire. In November, a fire boiled and roared across the brown grass in the Claresholm area.[1] A rampaging wind forced the fire to spread to the north and east. Evangeline Warren saw the billowing smoke from 64 kilometres (40 miles) away as it raced to Little Bow River.

Everyone who was available helped fight the fire, including women, who not only provided lunches but also carried water and sacks, and watched the horses of those working at the fire line. Cowboys from at least ten ranches became firemen. Despite their phenomenal efforts, flames continued to shoot 6 metres (20 feet) into the air. Finally, the government fireguard slowed the fire. The Little Bow River also served as a natural fire barrier, and as the winds diminished, those battling the blaze managed to gain control.

The next day the wind returned, sparking flames back into life. Within five hours, the fire had spread to the Picture Butte area north of Lethbridge, where it seemed to come to a stop. Once more, however, fire regained the upper hand. Beaten by the flames, ranchers began working to protect their own spreads. They ploughed better fireguards near buildings and moved their livestock to a more protected area across river. Despite the hard work of the settlers, the fire devoured vast blocks of pasture and farmland, and levelled the barns of the Circle Ranch.

In 1906, tragedy followed tragedy in the Red Deer River area. A bad fire moved from farm to farm that fall, burning off huge farming and pasture areas. The fire made short supply of the hay; deep snow and winter temperatures dipping to -52°C (-60°F) made foraging impossible for the livestock. Many farm and wild animals died.

The years from 1907 to 1910 were drought years. New Norway, located in the rolling prairie of central Alberta, was only one of many areas facing a fire threat in 1907. On the McIntyre homestead, men fought a fire using a wagon loaded with a barrel of water and sacks. In the meantime, Mrs. McIntyre packed what was most important to the family—food, significant papers, and keepsakes—in another wagon. Then she and her daughter pulled about 30 metres (100 feet) into a slough with their treasures and waited. Somehow, the men were able to save their house, but the inferno had forced the family to recognize and save what was truly essential to them.

When people knew that fire was about to strike, there was too much to do for even the most conscientious person to reduce all the risks. As a 1908

*On 20 April 1892, a ferocious fire spread from Gleichen, near Calgary, to Red Deer's edge. Every able-bodied resident in the village fought to save the community.* Red Deer Museum and Archives

fire approached his homestead in Weyburn, Saskatchewan, Arthur Finch re-ploughed and widened the fireguards around his farm and haystacks. However, he forgot the small piles of straw stacked just outside the fire-guard. They had been used for smoke smudges against mosquitoes the previous year. The advancing fire lit the old straw piles, and burning straw was carried away by the wind. A neighbour, arriving to help, saw the danger immediately. Without a thought for his own life, he went into the smudge piles to beat them out and saved the day for the Finches.

The Allens ranched near Wood Mountain, Saskatchewan. According to Mrs. Allen, fire was a yearly occurrence and a yearly curse. The Destroyer threatened survival for people and animals alike. To save themselves, wild animals ran from fire, and sometimes hundreds of rabbits could be seen scurrying in front of the flames.

Responsible not only for their own lives but also for those of their domestic animals, farm families almost always remained on their land, making frenzied preparations as fires bore down on them. On one occasion, hoping to save haystacks, Mrs. Allen took the blankets from her bed, wet them down, and circled the stacks with their scant protection.

*Smudge fires, used by settlers to keep mosquitoes and other insects away from livestock, could cause grass fires accidentally.* Glenbow Archives NA-4175-4

Another time, with her husband away, Mrs. Allen emptied the well to soak the winter feed. Then she turned out the livestock so they would not meet their deaths trapped in corrals. Other than that, there was nothing she could do for their safety. When her husband pulled into the yard some time later, the wheels of his wagon were aflame. He drove his team right into the kitchen so that his frightened horses would stand quietly, unable to see behind them while he extinguished the flames.

During the worst of the fire years, conflagrations showed many different faces. People's fears took many different forms, too. People would fear for their lives, family, friends, and home, or for their livelihood, livestock, and land. As hard as people battled against the enemy, they often suffered feelings of helplessness. Yet, rising up against the enemy were the unflagging spirits of the people.

## Fire Guardians

The NWMP were the first, and for some years, the only fire guardians of Western Canada. They investigated the causes of blazes and laid charges against those who purposefully or carelessly set fires. They also had the legal power to call anyone out to fight infernos. Refusal to obey their orders could result in fines.

In 1904, in the district of Alberta alone, Mounties investigated twenty-six fires. By then officially named the Royal North-West Mounted Police, they laid charges for twenty-three of the blazes, and the resulting fines amounted to $513 plus costs.[2]

With the growth of settlements, councillors for Local Improvement Districts also became *ex officio* fire guardians who could call on people to fight fires. Like the police, councillors were expected to take a leadership role in organizing fire-fighting efforts. Volunteers were also appointed to the position. In 1904, that gratuitous service was offered by 245 people on the prairies.

## Fireguard Trail

Pioneers valued roads, not just as the best path to town or the neighbour's place, but also as fireguards. A good, wide road could stop an oncoming prairie fire. If grass was left to grow tall along the right-of-way, fires easily jumped roads, but ploughing or controlled burning along the roadside let the divisions provide some protection. As a result, it was not unusual for roads to double as fireguards. Surprisingly, at least one seemingly endless fireguard became the best road west to Calgary.

*Ploughing fireguards was heavy and time-consuming work. It was sometimes necessary to plough guards during emergencies, and as a result, firemen staged ploughing contests to hone their skills.* Glenbow Archives, *Calgary Herald* Print File, Fire Department

The Alberta and Saskatchewan governments considered the fire risk so great in areas of the Palliser Triangle that they paid for the ploughing of enormous fireguards. A portion of one such fireguard was the 58-kilometre (36-mile) dividing line between Townships 24 and 25 in Alberta.[3] The guard stretched from Nose Creek, near Calgary, to Dead Horse Lake, about 80 kilometres (50 miles) to the east. In nearby communities, it was called the Fireguard Trail.

Much of the fireguard was first ploughed in 1907. Eight-man crews worked on the guard, which was 3 metres (10 feet) wide. Crews included a cook, a boss, and the men who drove the teams. Six teams of four horses each worked side by side to make the original guard. They ploughed to the Red Deer River, turned, and ploughed back to Calgary. Each of the teams pulled four double ploughs capable of clearing an eight-furrow width. When the Fireguard Trail was re-ploughed in 1908, 1909, and 1910, the government hired local farmers to do the job, and each worked an 8-kilometre (5-mile) stretch.

Settlers found the Fireguard Trail was a great roadbed for hauling coal, and after fences were strung across the range, ranchers used the trail for moving cattle. Sometimes as many as one thousand head of cattle were herded along the fireguard toward new pasture or the stockyards.

For the first Calgary Stampede in 1912, people drove their cars and wagons along the trail; eventually, the fireguard became the main route to Calgary. It was extended as far as Medicine Hat, and schools were built every 6 kilometres (4 miles) along the way. Then, in 1927, with the completion of Highway Number One, traffic along the fireguard began to decline.

However, all fireguards were important for safeguarding communities. Not only were they the last line of defence for towns like Carstairs, Alberta, they also provided employment. In Carstairs, eighteen men and their teams worked for a week to plough the guard, and every year, it had to be ploughed again.

## Railroading the Railway into Action

Most settlers of the western prairies arrived via the Canadian Pacific Railway. Completed in 1885, the CPR brought settlers farther and farther west with the completion of each stage of its development. Newcomers piled themselves and their effects onto railcars and stepped off the train at whatever station was closest to their destination. When it came to hauling their grain and livestock to eastern markets, the CPR and other rail lines were heroes.

When it came to prairie fire, however, the railways with their steam locomotives were villains according to ranchers and settlers. The battle over responsibility for grassland fires began shortly after the arrival of the rails. At the time, it was led by early stockmen such as General T. Bland Strange. Soon Native people on reserves were adding their voices to the protest.

One of the most vocal Natives was Chief Crowfoot from the reserve near Gleichen, Alberta, in the heart of the fire belt. The Blackfoot there had given permission for the CPR to cross reserve land. After the deed was done, the band learned the iron horse did not just bring people and trade goods to their land but also devastation. Crowfoot protested to the CPR, saying he had not been told of this potential consequence. He demanded compensation because the fires drove away the game. Since the Blackfoot were no longer at liberty to move to more plentiful hunting grounds, fires were contributing to their starvation.

Others also protested, writing letters and petitions. As early as 1894, citizens of Moose Jaw, in the Saskatchewan district of the NWT, were demanding that the government make railway companies provide fire patrols and plough fireguards on both sides of the tracks along prairie lines.

Some protestors simply expressed concerns over the railways' careless practices. Others laid charges with the Mounties against the rail companies.

One such charge was laid in September 1909. On a Friday afternoon, flames started near Phippen, Saskatchewan. Two Mounties, Corporal French and Constable Smith, called out about two hundred men to fight a fire that eventually burned a swath 3 kilometres (2 miles) wide and 16 kilometres (10 miles) long.

For local farmers, the damage was extensive. The fire blackened ripe crops, levelled haystacks, flattened three barns and one house, and claimed the life of one horse. Having lost essential parts of their livelihoods, the farmers were not about to let the culprit, CPR engine Number 188, avoid responsibility. Like others before them, the farmers took action and went to the Mounties to lay a claim against the railway.[4] However, proving fault was difficult, and cases sometimes stretched on for years.

By 1903, pressure groups had convinced the Canadian government to acknowledge the scope of the fire problem in the West. They had also effectively made their case concerning the role of railway locomotives in starting fires. According to settlers, ranchers, and townspeople, sparks in the black smoke from coal-burning engines fired the prairie. In addition, careless dumping of ashes along the tracks or rights-of-way spread fires. Even sparks generated when brakes were applied on the rails created danger.

The *Railway Act* of 1903 placed the responsibility for protecting the public from these fires directly on the railways; this included protecting victims from loss due to the fire.[5] Also implied in the legislation was the possibility of compensation. The act required companies to use protective appliances on locomotives, forcing them to put screens on their smokestacks and grates on their furnaces. It also made companies responsible for clearing the rights-of-way along the tracks so that tall grass and trees did not grow in the immediate danger zone. Not only were these access points to be cleared, fireguards were also to be ploughed and maintained along the rail line.

The legislation was amended and expanded in 1909 and 1911. Reenacted in 1912, the *Railway Act* was the most detailed on the continent in terms of fire. The most surprising and progressive clause required companies to have fire rangers patrolling the line. Locomotive fuel was also subject to restrictions, and burning lignite coal was prohibited. Locomotives had burned huge amounts of the soft, poor quality coal. This generated large piles of ash that had to be dumped along the way, and fires spread from dumping sites.

Compensation was also a strong principle within the act. Once it was proven the railway had caused a fire, victims could sue for enormous settle-

*The Canadian National Railway ploughed this fireguard in 1915. After a long battle with the railways, settlers won their fight for legislation that made railways responsible for the fires caused by their locomotives and for fire prevention.* Saskatchewan Archives Board R-A9770-4

ments. Not surprisingly, railway management became very serious about fire prevention.

Despite its bad reputation, the railway was not always the antagonist when fires broke out. Often, it was an important ally for prairie settlers. In Calgary's devastating fire of 1886, the CPR helped in the fire-fighting effort by providing a locomotive and tank car to haul water from the railway reservoir to fire fighters. Again, during an October fire in 1899, near the district of Dauphin, Manitoba, section hands from the railway fought hard to help defeat the fire foe.

The railway companies also helped in other ways. In towns with insufficient water supplies for extinguishing blazes, fire fighters could always hook their hoses to the railway water supply at the station. If flames raged in or near small prairie communities, the CPR would provide flatcars to haul fire engines from larger centres that owned better fire-fighting equipment. Of course, local volunteers had often already extinguished the flames by the time an engine arrived, but the goodwill effort on the part of the CPR was very significant.

## *Towns Take Precautions*

Prairie towns were equally intent on fighting and preventing fires, and on being compensated when fire took its toll. In the heart of the Palliser Triangle fire belt, Lethbridge often faced the fiery foe. The town was subject to strong winds and lightning storms. It received little precipitation in summer and minimal snow cover in winter. Meeting the town's water needs was also problematic. Waterworks for pumping the precious commodity from the river up the coulees to homes and businesses were expensive, and it took years to raise enough money to build them.

Lethbridge faced other exceptional circumstances, too. It was a wooden town, and coal was mined on the outskirts. Mine explosives were a necessary fire hazard, and slag smouldered at the top of many coulees. In addition, Lethbridge suffered the usual fires as a result of ill-fitting stovepipes and accidents with coal oil lamps.

For Lethbridge, the problems and risks associated with fire were substantial, but from early in its history, its people were concerned and progressive. As early as 1891, town council passed fire-protection laws. Inspectors could require fire-prevention action from building owners. No one could store straw, hay, or other flammable materials within the town limits unless they were covered properly or sufficiently isolated from other buildings and property. Every building where fires were used had to have at least one brick or stone chimney. For new construction, no building could have a stovepipe running through the roof or an outside wall. How stovepipes were to be secured and chimneys were to be constructed was also detailed.

At any one time, neither individual people nor corporations could possess more than 45 kilograms (100 pounds) of gunpowder or two cases of cartridges. Large quantities of other explosives had to be stored at least 182 metres (600 feet) from habitation and in buildings or magazines used only for that purpose. Ashes from households and businesses were not to be dumped in streets or yards, but rather in a pit or building designed for them. Any ashes from engines and locomotives were to be properly soaked. Violating any of the by-laws meant fines ranging from $5 to $100.

In addition to passing laws, town council decided to spend $1,425 on a chemical fire engine and raise $10,000 to build a fire hall. The town already had a fire bell. Taken from the wreck of the steamer *Alberta*, permanently docked at Lethbridge, the bell doubled as curfew bell for many years.

Although the town had a chemical engine by March 1892, one fire claimed four downtown buildings, including two that were used as saloons.

*Access to water was an enormous problem for communities in the Palliser Triangle. Water wagons, such as this one used in Medicine Hat, were used to deliver water to homes, spray streets for dust, and to carry the water needed to fight fire in parched prairie towns.* Medicine Hat Museum and Art Gallery PC12.1

*Prince Albert, Saskatchewan, purchased its first gasoline engine for fighting fires in 1904. Here, the engine is shown pumping water from the river and transporting it, by hose, to where it was needed.* Saskatchewan Archives Board R-A4340-2

Skeptics were critical of the chemical engine, but it had helped to prevent the spread of the fire, as had covering adjoining buildings with wet blankets. Two of the levelled properties, one valued at $1,000 and the other at $1,200, were not insured. The other two were insured significantly below their replacement value. Arson was suspected as the cause of the fire.[6]

In 1895, the torch of an arsonist became the proven cause of a downtown fire. A local tailor had convinced his mistress to fire the shop. Their plan had been to collect the insurance money and run off to get married. Not surprisingly, the law got in their way.

Like other prairie towns, Lethbridge progressed from bucket brigade to volunteer firemen to paid firemen. Still, trained manpower wasn't enough. The town wanted insurance against financial ruin on properties owned by the municipal government. The 1907 list of itemized insurance rates told the story of fire risk in Lethbridge. The basic rate was $.25 per year. Additional rates included:

Conflagration hazard $.25
Streets not paved $.02
Waterworks not standard $.03
Pump house not standard $.01
No pump house protection $.02
No valve for stand pipe $.05
Hose not sufficient $.03
No Salvage Corp $.08
Fire hall exposed $.02
Brigade not standard $.10
Horses work on streets $.01
No fire alarms $.05
High winds $.10
Single circuit from electric light station to pump house $.03

The total cost of insurance was $.80 for the year.[7] By comparing rates, it can be seen that the insurance company thought the problem of strong Lethbridge winds was ten times the problem of the horses or the inadequate pump house. Lethbridge's risk of fire was high, so the town was charged the same basic insurance rate paid by other Canadian towns, plus an equal amount to cover the added risk.

Lethbridge was serious about fire prevention, and newspaper coverage was common. In the summer of 1909, new by-laws required all two-storey buildings to have fire escapes and a water standpipe for fire department use. Doors were to swing outward. Spittoons were to be made of metal and not filled with sawdust, in case smokers threw matches and cigarette butts into them. In all, twenty recommendations were published for keeping towns-people safe from fire.

By the 1930s, Lethbridge also had a fire box alarm system. Even after new-fangled telephones arrived on the scene, firemen still had more faith in the fire box alarms. However, eventually the technology of telephones showed its potential as a weapon against the ancient enemy.

In 1936, for the first time in the Lethbridge area, a fire was spotted from the air. A Trans Canada Airline pilot saw fire in a wheat field and was the first to raise the alarm.

The Depression brought a strange development in the fire department's history. Money was tight, but according to provincial legislation, towns as large as Lethbridge had to have firemen for both day and night shifts. The night shift worked from 6:00 PM to 8:00 AM, but as far as the mayor was concerned, the night shift was being paid for playing pool and cards, or reading until the men went to bed. In 1929, the night shift had responded to fifty-four alarms although two-thirds were at the very beginning or end of the shift. In total, the night shift had spent sixteen hours fighting fires. That was not acceptable to the mayor, and he indicated that he wanted each man to do four hours of police duty on the night shift.

However, in Lethbridge, fear of fire was of even more concern than money matters. If an inferno threatened, there was no way the residents of Lethbridge wanted their firemen off fighting crime. Better they dreamed sweet dreams. At least then they would be available to save innocent victims from the fire fiend.

For Lethbridge, like other prairie towns, the development of fire-related by-laws and practices, and the growth of a professional fire department had uncertain and trying moments. However, fire danger was ever present, and cooperation and organization were the keys to fighting the madness.

## *Damage Control—Organized Confusion*

When fires raged in rural areas, an immediate response from neighbours was essential, but before telephones were common, organizing that response was difficult. Rural people didn't practise responding to fire alarms. They had no specialized equipment or assigned jobs. Yet somehow, prairie people always managed to mount a surprisingly united front against the foe.

Virtually no rain fell in southern Alberta from 1 April to 1 September 1910. Crops only sprouted in damp areas, and even these had withered and

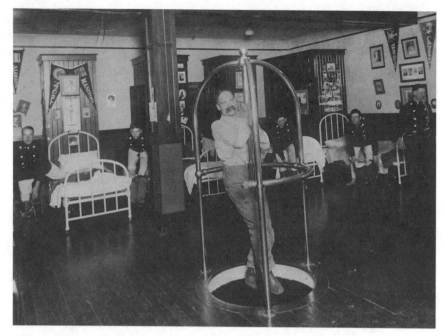

*This is the second floor dormitory at Fire Hall Number 7 in Calgary, Alberta.*
Glenbow Archives NA-2854-126

died. Fires sprang up everywhere. A man would be fighting a fire at his neighbour's place one day and a new one at his own place, the next.

One such fire began in early May at the mouth of Pickle Jar Creek in Kananaskis Country. A government survey party had camped there, and sparks from their campfire were picked up by the wind. Jumping across the Highwood River, the blaze burned on both sides of the water as it moved toward the grassland.

Numerous ranches were in the path of the fire. Despite a plea for assistance, no significant help was offered by the federal government. Only one man was sent from Ottawa to organize the fire-fighting efforts, and he knew nothing about prairie fires.

As they had always done, ranchers organized their own defence. They set up fire-fighting headquarters with two major command posts, one at the Bar U Ranch and the other at the Riley and Thomson Upper Ranch. Jobs, equipment, shifts, and attack locations were not left to chance.

Dan Riley recalled, "All sorts of primitive but effective measures were used. We set backfires, ploughed fireguards, established lookouts to warn of fresh outbreaks."[8]

Men ploughed fireguards while the fire pressed toward the Old Man River. Everyone moved as quickly as possible, but the ploughing was slow work. In one instance, to gain speed, mounted riders tied lariats to a plough and assisted the team of horses. Another man ploughed with a six-horse team. Given the tremendous horsepower, the man lurched into the air when his plough hit stumps, but as soon as he landed, he was back at work.

At the Gardiner Ranch, a deep mat of old grass fuelled the fire as it spread across the hills. There, fifty Stoney Indians fought the blaze, battling the flames at night, and catching what rest they could during daylight hours.

Women were also an important part of the effort. Their job was feeding the tired, hungry crews. In the hot kitchens, roast after roast was cooked. Hot meals and sandwiches were served at the ranches, and wagonloads of grub were taken to the fire lines. The men ate so much that an entire steer might be devoured in a few days. At the end of a shift, men would return to the ranches, dead tired. Once fed, their exhausted horses waited for the next shift, while the men looked for a place to sleep.

"... every foot of space was occupied by played out cowboys, snatching a few hours rest before going out on shift again. You couldn't put your foot down without stepping on a leg or arm ... So we grabbed a pair of blankets and were thankful to bed down in the corral. Anyways we never did make use of a bed for three weeks."[9]

Meanwhile, at the Bar U, Herb Millar and his men were desperately trying to save the huge pasturage needed by the ranch for livestock. They managed to plough fireguards on every side except one, where a big hill rose. Normally, no one rode up the hill because its steep grade was too hard on the horses, but the hill was definitely an access point for fire.

Strong, muscular, prize-winning Percherons were the pride of the Bar U. Millar harnessed a team and urged the horses up the steep grade. The huge animals strained. They heaved and struggled uphill. Behind them, the sod opened into a furrow. Up and up they surged until they had created a fireguard for the pastureland.

With shifts working day and night, eventually ranchers had fireguards stretching from the Highwood River to the Old Man River. In three weeks, the progress of the fire on the prairie was halted. The worst was over, but the fire had covered about 777 square kilometres (300 square miles) of timberland and prairie.[10] Still, ranchers stayed on guard. Where the grass was deeply matted, embers could hide beneath the surface and again be fanned into flames by the wind, so wagon patrols with barrels of water remained watchful. Others began the monumental job of cleaning up. Cattle and

*These people gathered to fight a grass fire near Lethbridge, Alberta, around 1912. Famous for its gale-force winds, Lethbridge was plagued by fires that were said to run in the wind at speeds faster than locomotives or galloping horses.* City of Lethbridge Archives and Records Management P19760212105

horses had died. For those that had been saved, cowboys hauled hay from areas that had not been hit by fire. A trainload of hay arrived from Okotoks, but without pasture, much of the livestock had to be moved out of the blackened landscape anyway. Meanwhile, burning continued in the valleys to the west, and as it was still early in the drought-stricken year, fires sprang up elsewhere on the prairies.

# CHAPTER SIX

# In Harm's Way

Many settlers faced fire far from the help of others. On isolated ranches and homesteads, families stood together, yet alone, in the path of infernos. When conflagrations approached, everyone, every possession, every dream was at risk. People of varied backgrounds suddenly became fire fighters. Not only men but also women battled flames heroically. When all hope had disappeared, their only option was to find a safe spot and watch the Destroyer do its work. At times, conflagrations left dozens—even hundreds—homeless on the newly settled prairie where there were few places to find shelter.

*Many settlers faced fire soon after they moved to the prairies. In 1906, the possessions of J.J. Gulley, a settler from Ontario, burned in this rail car near Innisfree, Alberta.* Glenbow Archives NA-2412-13

## No Place Like Home

The story of the Wilkins family reveals the bravery and perseverance of countless settlers who made their homes in the land of fire. Both Mary and her husband, William, immigrated to Canada from England. William was the self-assured type, enjoying challenge, and after serving in the Boer War, he set out for Canada, making his dream of homesteading in the Canadian West come true. After reaching Regina, he walked another 97 kilometres (60 miles) to find his quarter of land, situated near South Qu'Appelle along the Touchwood Trail, an area repeatedly hit by fire.[1] Dotted with poplar and willow, it was perfect for raising a family. Farming the land with his brother, Leo, made the venture easier.

In 1904, Mary arrived with their two children, an infant and a toddler. She had not been prepared for the primitive lifestyle that awaited her, and with no female companionship in the first year, she suffered terrible loneliness. In contrast, William and Leo had little time for loneliness. They were kept busy ploughing fields and building a small house, stable, barn, and outhouse.

In 1905, William faced his first prairie fire when he helped extinguish the flames at another settler's shack and stable. Battling a whole day and into the night had been backbreaking work. As he beat the flames with wet sacks, he seared his eyebrows, and the smoke pained his eyes. The heat rising from the burned ground was almost unbearable. Realizing the power of fire, he ploughed two fireguards around his own home as soon as he returned. He checked them often.

In the late spring of 1906, the Wilkins' third daughter, Sylvia, was born. Mary and the girls fared well throughout the summer. The fall crop looked good; it would be the first that William and Leo could sell. In September, William bagged the harvested grain, and leaving Leo, Mary, and the three children behind, departed for the grain elevator.

While returning home, he smelled fire in the air. This worried him. A crop still stood in his field, waiting to be harvested, and in the dry autumn weather, it could easily catch fire and threaten his family and home. He flogged his horses, and when he sighted poplars and shrubs on fire, a sense of panic filled him. He hurried the sweat-lathered horses through wedge after wedge of flames, and at times, they were completely surrounded by fire. Finally, he saw the farm. It seemed untouched when he thundered into the yard.

As the fire was nearing the Wilkins' farm, Leo and Mary had begun their frantic work. Leo gathered empty sacks, which he and Mary soaked in a tub of water. Ready to wage their battle and enduring the heavy smoke, the two cleared anything that could fuel the fire from around the house. The ploughed fireguard offered some protection. Still, fires could jump guards.

Mary's helpless children stayed inside, but if necessary, Mary and Leo would carry them into the middle of the slough as their final refuge. In the meantime, Mary and Leo tackled the flames.

When William pulled into the yard, the fire was less than a kilometre away. Mary's skirt was hitched to her waist. In one hand were matches to start backfiring; in the other was a wet sack to beat at the flames she was about to light. William ran to her, and for an instant, they held each other while Mary sobbed. With no time for emotion, they bent their backs to the work. Only when the fire finally veered away was there time to feel and hear.

With their work completed, William and Mary headed for the house. William fed the older girls a supper of bread, jam, and milk, while Mary snuggled Sylvia against her. She sat in the rocking chair where she had nursed each of her babies. This time, however, she had no milk. Her breasts were tight and hard.

Mary smelled the acrid smoke on her own clothes and body, and her mind filled with terrifying images. She knew she must shut out the fear to

*Tarpaper shacks provided temporary shelter for many early prairie settlers. The strong paper kept out the wind, but ignited instantly during fires, quickly creating infernos.* Provincial Archives of Alberta, E. Brown Collection, B.4510

feed her baby. Eventually, Mary found some inner calmness, and as her milk came back, so did relief for her and the baby. Only when she went to bed that night did she allow the tears.

The next day, William and Leo went to survey the damage and returned to the house with boots blackened by the soot. Their faces were grim, and their words did not come easily. Instead of describing the devastation, they talked of the future. Fire made ploughing easier and soot was a good fertilizer. The land would be green once again.

Eventually, Mary went out to see the effects of the fire for herself. Dead badgers, coyotes, and antelope sprawled before her. Her new world was neither comfortable nor comforting. It was not green and lush like the England that she had left behind. Could she stay, would she stay and raise her little girls in such a cruel land?

She looked at the log home, which held the few possessions she and her family owned. Small though it was, she had fought hard to save it. For Leo, the house and the land were not enough. He had witnessed too much cruelty in the prairie landscape and announced he would return to England. The rest of the Wilkins family, however, were prepared to become people of the prairie, to accept the cruelty of the fires to make their dream come true.

## Images of Heaven and Hell

As a result of the Laurier government's strong immigration policy, people began arriving in Canada from dozens of countries. Railways carried many to western Canada, and soon the landscape was dotted with individual homesteads and small communities where people shared religious beliefs and cultures.

In 1906, a group of Romanians began homesteading in the Flintoft-Wood Mountain area close to Moose Jaw, Saskatchewan.[2] In all, eight Romanian families settled on land that stretched pleasantly in three directions and dropped to a lake on the fourth side. Of course, access to water was important, and the sandy shoreline would be a good place for children to play.

The families needed money to build their farms, and luckily, paid work as threshers was available in well-established communities. That August, the grass at Flintoft-Wood Mountain was almost waist high. Using scythes, the Romanian men swathed enough hay to feed their cattle for the winter. Then, all but three of them left to harvest elsewhere.

In their small, closely knit community, the women didn't have to be lonely while their husbands and older sons were away. As well as tending to

*Often immigrant men would leave their families, temporarily, to go haying or harvesting at established farms, to earn cash for building their own farms. Families left behind on isolated homesteads were at extreme risk from prairie fires.* Saskatchewan Archives Board R-D773-2

three men in their sixties and ten children under ten years old, the women had other ever-present responsibilities.

One evening, as the sun set, the blue haze of the horizon turned an intense and fiery red. The women had already learned that the unusual colour signalled fire. However, the men had not yet ploughed fireguards, and without the horses that had departed with the harvesters, creating a ring of protection at that late hour was impossible. Instead, the adults met to plan how they would protect themselves, the children, the livestock, and the hay that was winter feed for the animals.

Backfiring was dangerous and out of the question; it would require more adults than those present to control the purposefully sparked flames. The controlled fire could turn on them with a force as destructive as a wildfire. However, they noted that there was scant fodder for the flames where the men had already hayed. This observation formed the basis of their plan.

The next day, the women picked up scythes. Determined to cut the prairie grass around their village as close to the ground as humanly possible, they slaved away, cutting a 6 to 9 metre (20 to 30 foot) swath on three sides of their homes. They were protected on the fourth side by the lake, a last possible refuge in case of disaster. As soon as they had scythed the area, everyone raked hard, cleaning away the newly cut grass and the heavy mat of dead grass that had accumulated near the roots.

When a rider appeared in the village, the inhabitants gathered for news. The man spoke English. They spoke Romanian. Yet somehow, they understood each other. The village was in the path of a huge inferno.

The messenger took charge, since he had more experience with fires than the newcomers. He instructed the women and older men to haul bucket after bucket of water from the lake, until every barrel, tub, and container in the community had been filled. When the wind lessened that evening, the messenger also directed some backfiring.

Inevitably, the sky filled with smoke. Flames appeared on the horizon. Having done all he could, the rider left to warn and help the next village to prepare for the firestorm.

Throughout the night, the Romanians scarcely slept. Nervously, they monitored the enemy's approach. By midday, the new settlers began the last of their preparations. They tethered the cattle down by the lake and hauled their food, clothes, and bedding to the sandy shore. They caught the chickens, put them in sacks, and carried them down the cliff to safety.

Leaving their young children at the lakeside in the care of the older children, the other adults returned to the village. They filled their buckets with water, doused everything, and hoped beyond hope that their lives and some of their hard won possessions would be spared. Finally, noise and smoke so completely filled the air that the women hurried down the cliff side to their children. The three men remained at the top of the cliff and watched the fire.

When the village was engulfed in smoke, the silhouettes of the men disappeared from the cliff top. The panicking women and children waded into the lake and prayed. Waist-deep in water, with dense smoke settling over them, they could barely breathe. Children who were old enough to understand put their faces in the water, raising their heads for gasps of smoky air and lowering them again for protection in the water. Other children were too young to understand the cool relief water would bring. All their mothers could do for them was bathe their tiny faces.

For twenty to thirty minutes, the fire raged at the top of the cliff above the lake. Eventually, the worst had passed. Still, there was no sign of the three men. Anxiously, the women waited for the air to clear. Finally, they saw human shapes on the shore. The older men had found shelter and protection at the base of the cliff. Relieved and thankful, the women and children waded from the lake toward them.

By then, evening had settled. To the adults, it seemed best to spend the night on the lake shore in the sheltered protection of the cliff. Just before sunrise, the survivors climbed to the flat land above. Stretching everywhere was the black soot of the spent fire. Fearfully, the men, women, and children made their way to the village. Amazingly, it had remained standing, as much a survivor as they were. Again thankful, the women cried. Then, joyfully, they began the trips up and down the cliff, returning their possessions to their rightful places.

It was another two weeks before the rest of the men returned from harvesting. With no way to communicate, they hadn't known about the perilous circumstances their families had endured. For the harvesters, the first sign of disaster was the burned-over land they travelled on the journey home. Fearfully, they hurried to the village and the arms of their families. The Romanians would never discover how or where the fire had started, although there were rumours that it had been sparked more than 240 kilometres (150 miles) away in northwest Montana.

In the end, the exact details of the origins of fires mattered less than the experiences of the people who fought them and survived. During their battles with fire, settlers proved time and time again the measure of the men, women, and children who made western Canada their new home.

## To Save Them All

For women with many dependants, simply deciding where to wage the battle against an approaching fire fiend could be almost impossible. In 1909, a farm woman living near Hannah, Alberta, was faced with that very dilemma.[3] This woman carried a heavy load. The eldest of her three children was only five, and she was pregnant again. Despite this, she cared for her father, who lay paralyzed in bed following a stroke. Also sharing the family home was the children's uncle and a cousin.

On an ordinary October morning, the farm woman's husband and the children's uncle left to help a neighbour build a sod house for the winter. As the day progressed, the wind came up, and the sky darkened as if a storm was blowing in. By noon, the smell of fire was noticeable, and one of the children saw flames in the southwest. The pioneer woman immediately began hurried preparations.

Unfortunately, she couldn't lift her father and carry him to safety. However, she did take the children to the safest spot within the fireguard, which was near the horse trough. Gathering blankets, she soaked them in the trough and wrapped them around the children. Then she warned them to stay where they were, no matter what happened. Grabbing another wet blanket and a pail of water, she returned to the house where her father lay.

Her children had as much protection as she could give them, but her father would die if the fire reached the grass near the house. Determined to save her disabled father, the desperate woman flailed at the flames. She was still extinguishing burning embers when the men and their wagon thundered into the yard. Although she was exhausted, she was thankful all her loved ones were still alive.

## *Dream to Heartbreak*

Sometimes pioneers were victorious against their fiery foe; at other times they were victims of tragedy. For one family, a 1909 fire in central Alberta brought unimaginable suffering. That spring, the three Grover brothers had emigrated from North Dakota to the Leo-Halkirk area. Earl was a bachelor, but Frank and Sam were married. Frank and his wife, Annie, had six children ranging from two to ten years old. Sam and Erma also had two children. The families quickly built homes, and during the fall, the men went threshing near Gadsby to earn some much-needed extra cash. Taking her children, Erma went with the men to work in the crew's cook car; Annie and her children stayed behind on the homestead. Fortunately, Annie's nearest neighbours, the Burress family, were only a half kilometre away should she need help.

On 29 September, the neighbour, Mr. Burress, and his son, Edward, were away digging coal near Sylvan Lake where, it was believed, a huge fire leaped into life. However, the women and children left behind knew nothing of the impending disaster. In fact, they were having a pleasant time. Mrs. Burress had taken her younger son, Herbie, to the Grovers' to celebrate four-year-old Kathleen's birthday.[4]

The grass that year was tall, heavy, and dry, lighting instantly when sparked by burning debris. Reaching speeds of up to 97 kilometres (60 miles) an hour, the wind blew burning boards from buildings and blazing tops from haystacks, spreading fire in all directions.

As soon as the two women saw the billowing clouds of smoke, they realized the magnitude of the approaching fire. Their only hope was to take the children to the Burress's place. Surrounded by ploughed fields, their house was protected, and the horse trough was filled with water, so the women could wet sacks for fighting flames if necessary.

Telling the four eldest children to run as quickly as possible to the Burress's house, the women followed with the younger Grover children— Kenneth, Kathleen, and Dorothy. Mrs. Burress carried Kenneth, and Annie moved the tiny girls along. Suddenly, Annie realized she had left her pocketbook at home. The $10 it contained was all she had left until her husband returned. She knew she had to go back, but Kathleen and Dorothy wouldn't continue on with Mrs. Burress.

Time was too precious to spend coaxing the girls to go with the neighbour. "You go on [and] look after the others. We'll catch up," Annie said.[5]

Mrs. Burress hurried ahead with the baby. By the time she reached home, her long skirt was burning. There, finding the older children safe, she doused her flaming skirt in the horse trough.

Annie needed only a few minutes to retrieve her purse. It turned out to be a few minutes too many, given the terrifying speed of her enemy. She tried to hurry her little daughters; she struggled to carry and pull them to safety, but the fire travelled more quickly than she could have imagined. The hungry flames overtook and engulfed them. When the fire had passed, Annie's little girls were small, charred bodies.

Distraught, Annie staggered to the Burress's yard. She was badly burned, and her two little girls were lying dead on the prairie. Although nothing could be done for the small victims, Annie was frantic, thinking the coyotes might further disturb them, and she asked Mrs. Burress to get them. Once she found her neighbour's children, Mrs. Burress brought them home and laid them out in the granary.

Another neighbour, aged seventeen, rode to tell the terrible news to Annie's husband, Frank Grover. He returned immediately with a doctor to treat her. There was little the doctor could do but try to ease the pain. Even that did not work. Annie's burned skin was hard, and the needles broke without delivering the blessing of a painkiller. Shortly after midnight, she died.

By the following evening, neighbours had brought three coffins from Stettler for the simple burial service. Time could heal the prairie, but life would never again be the same for the Grovers. As was so often the case when tragedy claimed the life of a mother during the difficult pioneer years, the surviving children were raised by their relatives.

What had caused the fire that led to this tragedy? No one knew for sure. A farmer creating a fireguard around haystacks was suspected of having started the wildfire when his planned burn got out of control, but charges were never laid.[6]

## *Work of the Godly*

In the spring of 1892, the very existence of Red Deer, Alberta, had been threatened by fire. Some considered it a blessing that the community had survived; others attributed survival to hard work. Again, in September of 1898, a traveller reported twenty fires had been sparked by the railway between Red Deer and Innisfail. With so many fires, early pioneers understood the threat they posed, and newcomers, including women and children, soon understood their duties.

Six such newcomers were nuns from the Order of the Daughters of Wisdom. Four were French and two were French Canadian. Their journey west had begun in September 1908. The French nuns had disembarked at New York and were later joined by the other two on a train from Montreal to Calgary.

All six nuns were young, enthusiastic, and anxious to create the best convent they could in the crude building that was to be their home in Red Deer. There was much to learn. The steep road up to the convent passed the tents of a Native encampment, and the nuns were interested to learn that the small fenced area beside it was an Indian cemetery. Equally interesting, but also more challenging, were the lessons of winter. Water pails on the stove froze solid during the night. Ill-fitting stovepipes meant wind blew smoke down and back into the convent. Good-naturedly the nuns claimed they were "being preserved, like hams and bacon, for long lives."[7] Then, in 1909, they were introduced to another prairie reality—fire.

On Holy Thursday, a fire had the audacity to rage toward the community's Catholic mission and convent. When Father Roncy saw the fire, he rushed to the convent to put the new nuns and the children who boarded with them on alert. They were to watch the fire closely while he went to warn others, and if it came too near, they were to fetch him immediately.

The scene outside was awe-inspiring. With the entire hill on fire, huge smoke clouds rolled toward them. The wind whipped up the flames, and by 2:00 PM, with the fire encroaching on convent property, the nuns and their charges went to work.

They drew water from the well and soaked the grass around the building. For two and a half hours, the women and children laboured against the prairie malevolence. Finally, the wind slackened, and the path of the fire ended at the edge of the soaked grass.

The nuns were happy they had been spared. Their Native neighbours were not happy. The next day, a group of Indians crossed the charred landscape and appeared at the door of the Catholic mission. Why, they asked,

*Sister Marie Agathe, Superior, and five other nuns arrived in Red Deer in 1908.*
*Within a year of their arrival, the Daughters of Wisdom found themselves fighting a*
*fire as it raced uphill toward them.* Red Deer Archives

had the priest burned the Native cemetery? Little did the nuns know that Natives were the ones most often accused of firing the prairie. This time, however, the Natives suspected religion had entered the delicate balance between fires used safely for purposes of good and fires set to accomplish some other goal, causing pain or hardship.

As time passed, the sisters built fireguards around the convent. One evening, the sky glowed with another large fire burning in the vicinity of the convent. However, the nuns decided they were likely not in the direct path of the fire and went to bed, trusting God would be their protector through the night. In the morning, the mission remained untouched by flames, and the Daughters of Wisdom were safe and secure.

## No Room in the Inn

When large numbers of dependent people were threatened by fire during the settlement years, finding temporary shelter for them was a serious challenge. Some adults were physically or mentally unable to help themselves during the chaos of fire, and in the aftermath, others took responsibility for their care. The thought that fire could threaten one of the few hospitals on the prairies for distressed and dependent adults was truly a nightmare. However, people in the path of fire often found refuge in unexpected places.

Brandon, Manitoba, lies at the eastern edge of the Palliser Triangle. As early as 1882, the town passed its first by-law concerning the prevention of fires. That same year, the city acquired a fountain-hose and steamer, as well as a hook and ladder truck for fighting fires. Usually, only people volunteered as fire fighters, but in Brandon horses also volunteered. With the sounding of an alarm, the first horses to arrive at the station were harnessed for duty.

By 1884, Brandon had acquired its first horse-drawn fire engine, a chemical soda and acid engine. The 1889 model was larger and needed two horses to pull it. The biggest problem, however, was water availability. Until 1892, Brandon did not have modern water works. However, water tanks 5.5 metres (18 feet) deep and 5.5 metres (18 feet) in circumference were located throughout the city. In terms of fire fighting in the early 1900s, the community seemed well prepared.

Then on Friday, 4 November 1910, disaster struck.[8] The temperature had plummeted to about -22°C (-7°F), and winds were strong. The Brandon Asylum, a hospital for mentally disturbed patients, was 2.5 kilometres (1.5 miles) out of town. It housed nearly 650 patients from all over Manitoba. The central building was twenty years old. With overcrowding a perpetual problem, other buildings had been added. Still, there wasn't enough room for everybody.

The local water supply was insufficient to meet the daily needs of the hospital, let alone for fighting fire. However, a better system of delivering water was in the works. By 4 November, new water hydrants had been installed, though not yet hooked up. The new system would pump 378 litres (1000 gallons) of water per minute, and staff looked forward to a greater sense of safety.

Shortly after 5:00 PM, about eighty staff were on duty when a fire started in the upper garret of the central building of the asylum. Flames rapidly spread to the roof. Whipped along by the wind, the flames lit up the night sky. The Brandon Fire Department rushed to the scene with its equipment, only to discover it was helpless. There was not enough water for the hydrants to halt the fire's spread. This endangered the lives of seven hundred people, most of them unable to fend for themselves.

While the entire hospital was being engulfed in flames, the staff, including guards and attendants, began the difficult evacuation of their patients. Since only staff members really knew the layout of the building and how to handle the patients, they returned to the burning hospital, again and again. They remained as calm and orderly as possible, to avoid upsetting the patients.

In the meantime, firemen did their best to control the fire. Ordinary people provided first aid to those who needed it, the police took the most dangerous patients to the police cells in town, and the militia watched over others, returning those who wandered from the group back to the fold.

When Chief Attendant McRae thought he saw one last patient still inside, he crawled through a fourth-storey window for the rescue. There was no one there, but before he could return to safety, the roof collapsed. With the dangers of smoke, flame, and debris around him, he struggled to another window. Luckily, a patient caught sight of McRae's figure at the window. He alerted firemen, who rescued McRae. The Chief Attendant owed his life to the observant patient.

Other patients had helped retrieve bedding, clothes, and furniture from one of the buildings, but at the height of the chaos, many patients seemed beyond control. Some yelled, screamed, and ran wildly from their protectors. As many as thirty patients went missing, either purposefully or in confusion. Yet, by the next day, only four patients were still absent, and eventually, they too were found.

The fire, itself, did not claim the lives of staff or patients. Yet, tragically, one of the women who wandered off in the confusion died of exposure near an ice-covered pond.

One problem in the immediate aftermath of the fire was housing 650 people on that cold, winter evening. There were no inns large enough to accommodate them, so barns were used as temporary lodging. As quickly as possible, livestock were led from the shelters, and the citizens of Brandon brought food and blankets for the comfort of the patients. However, caring for the patients and supervising them in barns presented an impossible situation. Even though some patients only suffered from impaired judgement, others were dangerous to themselves and their fellow patients.

Nowhere was there adequate room for the homeless, except in the Armoury and the Winter Fair Building. The buildings were quickly heated, furnished, and adapted for cooking and sanitation. In the end, these temporary homes served for two years while a new hospital was built.

Although, at first, a patient had been blamed for the fire, the actual cause was unknown. Eventually, the hospital administration claimed a live electrical wire had led to the conflagration. Luckily the fire had burned itself out

*About seven hundred patients and staff escaped from the 1910 fire at the Brandon Mental Health Centre in Brandon, Manitoba. After spending the night in barns, the patients walked into town, where the Armoury and the Winter Fair Building were the only places large enough to shelter them.* Provincial Archives of Manitoba N14991

before spreading into Brandon or across the prairies. Still, the story was sad twice over. First, the people who had been threatened by the fire were already victims of personal tragedy, and second, the number of patients who had been in the direct path of the disaster had been shockingly large.

The scarcity of water for fire fighting would pose a perpetual problem for prairie communities. However, like many other difficulties, this one would eventually become more manageable. Still, when fire threatened, it was usually the people willing to place themselves in harm's way for the sake of others who made the difference between life and death. Time and time again, whether flames raged as grassland fires, as conflagrations in parklands, or as infernos in wooden towns, dozens of individuals heroically battled the odds. Sometimes they lost, but other times they managed to save what was truly important—people.

# Childhood with the Fire Demon

For parents, nothing could be worse than the thought of their children being threatened by fire. Usually when children were endangered, their mothers, fathers, grandparents, or teachers were nearby to protect and reassure them. However, occasionally children found themselves alone when fires raged around them. Fear and panic would be their expected responses. Yet, as children on the prairies faced the terrible lessons taught by fire, some exhibited a heroism and understanding far beyond their years.

## Born In Fire

Rail travel made it relatively easy for women to join their husbands on homesteads out west. Given the small number of doctors and the great distances of many homesteads from the nearest towns, they often gave birth with little help from others. Frequently, there were no midwives or even neighbours to assist during the final stages of labour.

If expectant mothers were fortunate, their husbands helped them. Yet, lack of cash for basic necessities meant men were sometimes away at other jobs when their babies were born. Mothers recognized the peril of fire for both themselves and their newborns, but they could not alter the course of nature. So, if firestorms threatened when a mother went into labour, the smoky air and flames became the most terrifying of experiences.

One expectant mother, a Mrs. Haney, was alone when her labour pains began prematurely; at the same time a fire raced toward her home. Flames soon surrounded her house, where she was caught in the throes of childbirth. With no one to help her, the difficulties of childbirth would have been enormous under ordinary circumstances. Knowing that fire raged around

*On 24 December 1946, Janet McWilliams was 18 years old and on the verge of adulthood when she died tragically while sleeping in an upstairs bedroom of this Calgary house.* Glenbow Archives, *Calgary Herald* Print File, Fires 1945-1959

her made the initial stages even more trying. Trapped and hysterical, she went into the final stages of delivery.

Born prematurely in a smoky shack with no one to help its mother, the baby died. Weeks after the fire, Mrs. Haney also passed away. The cause was complications from the birth, a time when panic reigned and no one knew of her desperate need.

On another homestead, a Mrs. Erickson had gone full term when her life and the life of her newborn were threatened. At the time, her husband, Axel, was away doing an errand. The baby was born in his absence, and exhausted after giving birth, Mrs. Erickson and her baby stayed in bed and rested. A fire was burning nearby, and unaware of how much danger they were in, they waited for help to arrive.

Neighbour Tom Craig saw the fire as it approached the Erickson's. Knowing the family would need help, he headed for their house. Inside, he found the new mother and her tiny baby. Quickly, he carried the newborn a few hundred yards to a newly ploughed field. Leaving the baby there, he went back for Mrs. Erickson.

Craig returned to the house one more time to grab bedding for mother and child. As he did so, he saw an arm of fire spreading toward his own home. Still, he set about beating out the fire around the Ericksons' house. When Craig moved beyond the heavy smoke to gasp clean air, the good Samaritan watched his own home go up in flames.

About 1908 in the Killam district of Alberta, W.A. Rancier was away from his homestead during part of his wife's pregnancy. He had taken an extra job because the family needed the money, and he promised to be home two weeks before the baby's expected birth. When Mrs. Rancier saw the smoke of a distant prairie fire, there was no way to contact her husband. She could only wait and watch. Each day, the smoke came closer, and so did her due date. Her worry for her other tiny children intensified, but there was nothing she could do.

Already anxious and fearful, Mrs. Rancier went into labour with flames visible on the nearby ridge. A strong wind meant fire would soon descend upon her and her family. Doubled in pain, she gathered her toddlers near her and took to bed. Finally, baby Samuel Rancier was born to his exhausted mother.

As soon as she was able, Mrs. Rancier dragged herself to the window. The vision before her eyes brought joy and unimaginable relief. She had been doubly blessed. While she had endured the labour of giving life to her youngest child, the wind had shifted. The fire danger had roared off in a new direction, sparing the Rancier family and their home.

## Breath of Life

Three-year-old Samuel Harrison Mayhood arrived with his family in the Nosehill area near Calgary in 1889. The Mayhoods had left the moderate, moist climate of Ontario for the dry fire-prone climate of the Alberta foothills. As a child of the prairies, Samuel knew what to do during a fire. At the age of fourteen, he had already lived through two fires near his home.

The first fire had happened at the turn of the century. Because of the lack of precipitation the previous winter, a serious fire hazard had loomed since June. Luckily, Samuel's father had ploughed fireguards around their land, and although the fire burned all around the guarded area, their farm was not touched. However, the fire had been so hot, it had burned deep into the roots of the prairie grass, destroying the vegetation.

Despite the enormous area charred in this first serious fire near the Mayhood farm, the second proved more frightening to Samuel. A new immigrant had settled about 3 kilometres (2 miles) away. Intending to break land, he decided to burn the brush and matted grass to make ploughing easier. His fireguard was too small for the dry prairies; flames jumped the guard and raged out of control toward the Mayhood place.

Fourteen-year-old Samuel and his brother Fred were at home alone. With no one else to take charge, the boys quickly saddled their horses and set out to fight the fire where it was crossing a corner of their land. On their way there, the wind suddenly shifted, and the fire turned to race toward them. All the boys could do was gallop hard to outrun the enemy at their back.

Finally, Samuel and Fred reached a trail that acted as a fireguard, offering some protection to both the boys and their home. Behind the small guard, Samuel and his brother would be able to prevent the fire from jumping across it and approaching their home. Too, they could watch for burning manure lifted by the wind to be dropped elsewhere, possibly kindling a new blaze.

Little did the young boys realize that flames were not the only threat they faced from the approaching firestorm. The nearer it came, the more overpowering was the smoke. Caught in the midst of clouds of grey debris, the boys could hardly breathe, and the suffocating smoke grew thicker. Taking refuge in the dirt, the two teenagers pressed themselves as flat as possible against the ground. The fire passed, and the Mayhood boys were thankful they lived to tell their story.[1]

## *Of Childhood and Manhood*

Ideally, when children spent time with their grandparents, they would feel safe and secure. The lessons learned at a grandma's or grandpa's knee were casual ones, acquired in a relaxed atmosphere of love and support. For the Lifeso children, the lessons learned at their grandma's would remain in their memories for a lifetime.

Around 1911, the Lifeso family was farming in southern Saskatchewan near the Dirt Hills. Hay was plentiful in the Yellow Grass marsh, a few days' travel from their home. One day, Mr. and Mrs. Lifeso decided to go haying, so they left their two children in the care of their grandmother, who lived in a sod home on Gibson Creek.

In most places on the prairies there were not enough trees for building log cabins, so many settlers used sod instead. Sod homes were warm in winter, cool in summer, and quite dark throughout the year. They were usually temporary shelters, prettier than tar paper shacks, but not the houses the pioneers wanted or expected when they arrived in the land of their dreams. Still, many spent years in their sod homes, and the unusual houses did have certain advantages, especially when it came to fire.

A fire approaching from the Dirt Hills was visible for days during the Lifeso children's stay with their grandmother. Even at a distance, the flames created a spectacle of smoke. Overhead, the sun turned a fiery red, and the children became more and more curious, as well as more and more anxious.

Finally, the air around them filled with the smell of burning grass, willows, and tarpaper shacks. The children could no longer pretend they weren't afraid. Yet amazingly, despite the impending disaster, their grandmother managed to appear calm and reassuring to them.

"What can we do, Grandma? Will we burn up?" I [E.L. Lifeso] asked my grandmother as she walked from the door to window and back again. "Can't we go somewhere?"

"There's no place to go," she answered. "But don't worry. If the fire comes this way, it will burn right over our sod house. Maybe you could bring the dog and your cat inside now so they don't get scared and run away."[2]

The fire spread from the hills to the nearby hay flats, so the children were relieved when they saw two figures approaching on the horizon. As they neared the house, the men beat away the flames that had begun licking at whatever they could find in the ploughed land by the house. Yet, as amazing as it was to the children, their grandmother still remained controlled and purposeful.

While the two men slowly fought their way through the fire to the sod house, Grandma prepared tea and lunch for them. After they had beaten the nearby flames into submission, the men stumbled to the door. The children had never seen such scarecrows.

Their eyes were sunken and red rimmed in faces blackened by fire and smoke. Their hands were blistered, their shoes in tatters, their clothes just hung on their gaunt frames.

For the Lifeso children, seeing the physical appearance of the men who had secured their safety was a lesson they would not forget. It taught about the terrifying power of prairie fire and the unbelievable physical and mental strength required to fight the fire monster. The men's frightening and dishevelled appearance deepened the children's sense of dread, but it also spoke of the bravery required to fight fires.

Soon the fire fighters had finished their tea and sandwiches. The fire demon was still lurking around other homes, so it was time to press on. After words of thanks and goodbye were exchanged, the men left the children in the care of their calm and competent grandmother.

That same year, fire stalked a family known to the Lifeso children; they lived at the Stopping House, halfway between the Lifeso home and Moose Jaw. There, nine-year-old Norman was expected to help fight the fire. Like hundreds of other young boys during times of impending disaster, Norman was assigned a man's job. His task was to ride his pony, Dandy, and drag the newly slaughtered carcass of an old bull along the creeping fire line. The responsibility was formidable and frightening, even for experienced adult cowboys and cow ponies.

Norman and his pony rode the danger line and returned when Dandy could do no more. Assuming the boy might also need to be relieved of his frightening job, a cowboy asked if he was tired. Before the boy could reply, his father answered for him. "Hell no! Saddle another horse," Norman's father insisted.

To the Lifeso children, learning of their friend's experience was just one more life lesson in the land of flames. On the fire-threatened prairies, boys were expected to do the jobs of men, anytime they were needed. The questions of how a boy felt, what he thought, and what he wanted to do were seldom asked. Instead, a father could simply say, "Hell, no," and nine-year-old boys saddled fresh horses and became men.

## Good Old Golden School Days

For thousands of immigrants arriving in the Canadian West, the thought of fire trapping children in country schools was a terrifying one. Still, it sometimes happened. In September 1908, a school near Weyburn, Saskatchewan, was one among many to stand in the path of a fire fiend. September had been a dry month near Weyburn that year; most farmers had finished their harvest early.

At about 2:00 one afternoon, Olive Finch Fredeen and other farm children were working on their lessons at school. Outside, bits of white ash began falling from the air. Gradually, the smell of smoke filtered into the schoolroom, signalling an approaching fire. Unfortunately, like hundreds of recently constructed schools, the building had no fireguard.

By 3:00 PM, the teacher was seriously worried. He was prepared to stay and fight if the flames continued toward the school. He was also experienced enough to know that children should not remain in the path of danger; one man simply could not protect so many of them. Besides, many of the older children would be needed at home to fight the fire demon.

When the teacher dismissed the students, insisting they go directly

*Settlers built sod homes out of necessity on the treeless southern prairies.*
*Fire could not destroy sod walls and usually ran quickly across a sod roof.*
Glenbow Archives NA-1255-31

home, Olive and the others ran most of the way. The little girl was terrified, but her own home had good fireguards ploughed around it. Still, when she arrived home, she noticed her anxious father keeping watch and holding a wet gunnysack to beat back embers that jumped the guard. This time Olive's family was lucky; the fire passed and their home was safe.

At school, the situation was different. There, the teacher continued to beat at threatening flames. Nearby, a full granary, with a haystack tight against it, offered ample fuel for lurching flames. The teacher was powerless, and his only refuge was a ploughed field. Finally, he sought its safety and watched as the fire levelled the school, devoured the granary, and charred the surrounding area. The fire had spread over an area of 56 square kilometres (35 square miles) in less than a day.

The teacher's firm directions to his students had been good ones, although there were no guarantees that all had reached safety. He knew it had been more important to send them home than to keep them a few extra minutes to learn textbook lessons. Still, it had been a day for learning equally important lessons—especially about bravery—from their parents and other adults.[3]

## Childhood Terror

Some days were not to the liking of H. Holden. He lived about 40 kilometres (25 miles) from Herbert, Saskatchewan, and on a Saturday one October morning in 1915, his father left for town with a load of wheat. Later that day, when his mother realized their cattle had broken into the hay corral, she sent her eldest son and his eight-year-old brother, Mel, to chase them out.

The two boys set off to fix the fence with the tools they needed for the chore. The elder Holden boy was irritated about the cattle. There were all kinds of things he would rather be doing. Worse yet, the miserable west wind tore at the boys as they walked. They could barely make headway against it, but finally, the job was done.

As they headed home, the boys smelled smoke. Then, coming over a rise, they saw smoke billowing in the sky, a little to the west of their home. They had heard stories about fires and knew this one could trap their mother and baby sister. Instinctively, they started running home as fast as they could. As they ran, the boys watched the smoke become thicker and thicker around their home. Then, still 1 kilometre (0.6 miles) from home, they could see red tongues of flame lurking behind the house.

> We started to run harder. Then Mel fell. He shouted to me, "Run, you can make it." My whole world was falling apart … I might make it alone, but that would be the end of Brother Mel. [*sic*][4]

There was no way that the elder Holden would leave his brother behind to face the enemy alone. Instead he thought about creating a safe zone by backfiring. Unfortunately, he didn't have matches. In the distance, they could see the buildings of their farm silhouetted against a wall of flame. There would be no safety there; to continue home would be to die.

Nearby was a newly ploughed field belonging to their Uncle Shay. It was located downhill and sheltered from the wind. Dropping the fencing tools, the ten-year-old grabbed his brother's hand and pulled him toward what could be a safe haven. They were almost to the ploughed land when Mel stumbled and fell again, dropping his brother's hand.

> I picked up Mel and carried him a few steps and then put him down and took his hand and ran again. It would be close. Mel fell again and I jerked him to his feet. He was crying "I can't make it."

They rested just long enough to catch their breaths. The elder Holden boy felt tears in his eyes. Filled with self-pity, he suddenly realized that his muscles ached. They screamed in pain, but what did it matter? Even if they reached Uncle Shay's land and survived the fire, they might no longer have a family—no mother, no sister, and no father, if he too had been caught in the fire.

Desperately, Mel pleaded with his brother to leave him and run to safety. The ten-year-old refused, pulling his brother with him. Ahead of them, the fire closed in on the boys and encroached upon the stubble field. The smoke loomed so thick it seemed a palpable thing. "Will it hurt much?" Mel asked. His brother didn't know and didn't answer.

Suddenly, in the smoky darkness, the two boys ran into a fence. The ten-year-old knew where they were. Immediately he rolled and dragged his exhausted brother under the fence and into the furrows of the newly ploughed sod. The heat was searing as the elder boy pulled open a sod furrow, manoeuvred Mel into it, turned his face sideways, and pulled the turf over him.

Only then did the ten-year-old make a bed in the ploughed land for himself. Under the cover of soil, it was difficult to breathe. Smoke filtered through, and the heat seemed unbearable. From a slit in his sod blanket, he saw the fire shoot over him. When the flames had passed, the air cleared enough for them to breathe more easily. Exhausted and afraid of what might be, he and his brother stayed in their sod beds and finally fell asleep.

When the cold of dawn awoke the boys, they faced the day and whatever waited for them at home. Filled with dread, they set out on the last leg of their journey. Blackened fence posts smoked. The acrid fire smell was still strong in the wind.

As they approached their home, the boys' hearts swelled with hope. The house and barn remained standing. The horses were beside the barn, but their appearance brought home the horror of fire. "Their hair was burned off their hides and their eyes were right out of their sockets." However, there was also cause for celebration. The boys' father, mother, and baby sister were alive. The boys were safe and they were not alone.

In the immediate aftermath of the fire, the boys' father had the terrible task of shooting the horses. Years later, Mr. H. Holden, the elder of the two boys, reflected, "I believe that this was perhaps my first realization that death can be a friend."

The boys also learned of their mother's bravery. As protection against fire, the boys' parents had kept earth piled high against the walls of their house. Knowing her daughter Alma should be safe there, Mrs. Holden had secured the little girl so she couldn't run out into the fire. Then she had gone to the barn, where she stood guard with a pitchfork, tossing burning hay as far from the barn as she could. In the years that followed, despite the pain of their fire experience, the Holdens, like hundreds of other prairie people, continued to farm.

## Lessons for a Young Cowboy

In 1925, Philip Long was only thirteen years old. His father worked on the 76 Ranch, which extended along the White Mud River from Cypress Hills to the Montana border. Since it was first established by Sir Lister-Kaye in the 1880s, the ranch had been a frequent victim of prairie fires.

Part of the reason for the ranch's susceptibility to repeated devastation was its sheer size; it was still one of the largest ranches in the country. By the 1920s most of the 76 Ranch operation lay within four huge leases that stretched for about 322 kilometres (200 miles) and covered 101,175 hectares (250,000 acres). Situated as it was in the Palliser Triangle fire belt, one area or another often lay in the path of a wildfire.

One day, Philip drove the car to school. At the time, driving laws were less rigid than they are today, and many boys learned to drive at an early age, so they could help on farms and ranches. While at school, Long smelled smoke. He could see the grey clouds rising from somewhere near the centre of the ranch lease. Given the strength of the wind, the young boy knew every available hand would be required to fight the fire.

It was an unspoken rule that everyone—including students his age—dropped whatever they were doing and went to help fight fires. Realizing the car would be needed, Long approached his teacher for permission to leave. The teacher was young and recently arrived from the East. She flatly refused Long permission, accusing him of wanting time off from school. Frustrated, Long tried to make her understand. She stood her ground and became angry, refusing to listen to anything more about prairie fires.

Philip was in a bind. His mother and father would expect him to bring the car home, and he saw only one option—disobeying his teacher. When he told her again that he had to leave, she forbade him, indicating that if he left, he would not be welcome back at the school.

For a second, Long hesitated. Then he walked out of the schoolroom and drove home. Just as he had expected, his mother had food ready for her son to take to the men fighting the fire. Philip's job would be to drive the cases of canned tomatoes, sandwiches, coffee, cakes, and pies to the fire line, while his mother continued cooking. Philip also packed water containers to fill at the river. Then he added sacks and extra, old blankets to the load before he set out. He planned to drive the car across a low spot on the river to save time and headed directly toward the fire line.

Philip manoeuvred the car down the riverbank and up the other side. Ahead lay a blackened wasteland, still smoking in places. Conscious of the time it would take to drive around the smouldering landscape, he decided instead to continue straight across. From a hilltop, he could see flames straight ahead. He turned west and increased his speed. With the heavy smoke burning his eyes, he realized taking the shortcut had been more dangerous than he suspected. He drove up another hill and ahead loomed a wall of fire and smoke.

I was going downhill too fast to stop. There was only one thing to do. I pulled the throttle down and ducked my head as the world became a hot blast of smoke and fire. The car burst through the fire line and out into the open grass.[5]

From a few feet away, men who were fighting the flames looked up in astonishment, their faces covered with soot. Recognizing Philip, one of the farmers came alongside the vehicle. The man smiled, joked about being in Philip's way, and asked for a drink of water.

Philip finally reached the group that included his father. Mr. Long's face and hands were also black with soot, and Philip worried his father might have bad burns. Though ready to drop from thirst and exhaustion, the men in his father's group just grabbed something to eat and drink and then went back to the fight. When they had finished, Long's father directed him to set up a makeshift camp, where exhausted men could eat and rest.

Before riding back to the fire, Long's father looked down at him. "I'm proud of you, son," he said, and the words made the boy "feel like one of the men."

Seventy-eight men had come to fight the fire, and others continued to arrive. Some came in buggies, some on horseback, and some on foot. Long's was the only car, but other farmers had brought barrels of water on horse-drawn stone boats, so that sacks and blankets could be soaked.

Despite their strenuous efforts, the men were fighting a losing battle. As a last resort, Long's father called together ten cowboys, and they decided to sacrifice a horse so its carcass could be used to drag the fire line. Men on foot followed, using their sacks to beat out what flames remained. Two additional horses were sacrificed, and riders took turns at the dangerous and searing-hot task.

That afternoon and evening, Philip made three additional trips with the car to bring back food, water, and coffee. At sundown, the wind stopped, but about a hundred men continued fighting until all flames were extinguished. By the time it was out, the fire had burned an area about 19 kilometres (12 miles) long and 6 kilometres (4 miles) wide. Three horses had lost their lives, and 68 tonnes (75 tons) of hay were gone.

Eventually, Philip and his father spoke with the hayer who had started the fire. Apparently he had lighted a cigarette, and the match had fallen, landing in a hayrack piled high with dry fodder. While he tried to beat out the flames, the horses' tails caught fire. He tried grabbing the reins, but the team pulled them through his hands. As the horses galloped across the field, flames were ignited in their wake. The horses finally reached a slough and ploughed into it. Their lives had been saved, but in the meantime the entire field was ablaze.

Despite exhaustion and badly burned hands, the hayer had fought the inferno to its end. When they dropped the hayer off at home, Long's father made two simple statements that his son would long remember. "Don't worry about it any more," he said. "We all make mistakes."

The next day, thirteen-year-old Philip was allowed to sleep late. In the evening, his father took him to the teacher's home to explain what had happened. Once she understood what fire on the prairie really meant, Long was welcomed back at school.

# The Unexpected: Cause & Consequence

The exact cause and effect of individual fires cannot always be ascertained. Human firebugs create havoc. Petroleum deep beneath the earth's surface rises to become fuel for fire fiends aboveground. Grain elevators shed cascades of sparks and cinders as they crumple in ruin. Other buildings burst into towers of flame. On farms, controlled burns of garbage, weed patches, stubble, and smoke smudges rage out of control. Even the sky drops fireballs every now and again.

## Arson—The Unthinkable

With fire such an enormous threat on the prairies, it is unthinkable that people would set fires deliberately and take satisfaction from the resulting destruction, danger, and chaos. However, there have always been a few individuals who either were fascinated by fire and the havoc it created, or who wanted the insurance money.

Two of the communities hardest hit by arsonists in the past are located in Manitoba. Portage la Prairie fell victim prior to the turn of the century, and Winnipeg suffered an arsonist's siege in 1912. In both instances, special investigators were required to find the arsonists. For both communities, the extent of the damage was shocking.

In the 1880s, Portage la Prairie was a small community with a promising future, if it could only manage to weather the bad times it was experiencing. First a terrible fire took place on 18 January 1885, in -40°C (-40°F) weather. A stiff wind fanned flames, and despite volunteer efforts, the Presbyterian church fell.

Real problems began a year later on an evening in mid-December 1886.

The tower of the fire hall caught fire, and flames shot into the air. Volunteers risked their lives to save the team of horses that rushed men and equipment to fires, but Portage lost the rest of its fire protection, including 4572 metres (1500 feet) of hose, a hose cart, and a Ronald engine worth $3,500, when a good kitchen stove cost from $20 to $30. Unfortunately, the town's fire insurance had lapsed, and town council had no money to replace the engine.

The fire hall blaze was merely a harbinger of things to come.[1] Six days later a business block went up in flames and damage was estimated at $3,500. Then, in the desperate cold of New Year's morning, with no fire engine and scant water for fighting the fire, volunteers learned that Main Street was ablaze. Damages there mounted to $30,000. On 16 February, yet another building went up in flames. Once again, because of the cold weather and lack of water, the building was lost. The financially strapped community had suffered devastating damage over a short period of time. Citizens suspected an arsonist was on the loose, and the townspeople were terrified.

*In 1911, these Wainwright, Alberta, residents saw their town devastated by a fire that had started in the local poolroom.* Provincial Archives of Alberta A.2242

Destruction continued. On 6 April, flames licked at the Queen's Hotel, and on 12 April, the hotel's stable caught fire. The flames spread, levelling the stable and hotel, which were valued at $7,000. While fighting the hotel blaze, firemen learned of two additional fires, one on another town block and the other at the skating rink. In the middle of May, a log building by the Queen's Hotel burned to the ground.

By this time, local police knew they needed help to track the culprit. A reward was offered, and soon Detective Foster from Brandon, Manitoba, was hot on the trail of the arsonist. At last, the citizens of Portage were hopeful the reign of flames would end.

On 20 May, the local mill was set on fire, a fire that ultimately doomed most of Main Street and resulted in another $20,000 damage. Fire swept through another hotel; it was extinguished, but the same hotel was re-torched on two subsequent occasions. Fortunately, these fires were also discovered and halted before the building was in ruin.

The financial cost of the arsonist's work was so enormous, the town thought it might never recover. Although the lives of many had been threatened, amazingly, no one had died. Finally, Detective Foster found his man. In fact, he found the two men responsible.

The torched town had become too hot for Sam Mick, and he had tried to flee when he realized Detective Foster was onto him. However, the determined detective followed Mick and arrested him. Soon, Foster had also arrested Mick's drinking buddy, Jim White.

The tale of the town's torchers quickly unravelled. White had provided the necessary coal oil and paid Mick to set fires while he watched. Unbelievably, when the court learned that White had been under the influence of alcohol during these escapades, the judge allowed him to walk, leaving Mick as the fall guy. Mick was sent to jail for five years.

Although the damage to Portage la Prairie was shocking, the tale of a firebug in Winnipeg during 1912 was even more tragic. There, death followed in the wake of an arsonist's flames. His victims were the first two Winnipeg firemen to die in a fire, and eight spectators.

Chaos reigned on the night of the deadly fire. First, the arsonist set fire to a shack behind the CPR immigration office; then to a haystack; and next to a shed at a sash factory, where the deaths occurred. The captain and eight firemen were fighting the blaze as it crept toward two naphtha gas vats. Outside, hundreds of curious spectators gathered.

The vats exploded with all the power and deafening noise of a detonating bomb, vaulting bricks and debris into the air. Suddenly, two firemen were dead and four were injured. Five spectators, including a twelve-year-old boy, were also dead. Nine others were rushed to hospital, where three later died.

The police investigated, and the firebug was eventually arrested. His confession was startling: he had set more than two hundred fires![2]

## An Unexpected Explanation

The most unexpected cause of fire on the prairies was reported 9 October 1935. The following is the news report:

### Meteorite Fires Straw Stack
### Threshing Machine Saved by Quick Action of Men

Vegreville, Alta.—Rain and snow halted threshing operations on many farms, but the peak in astronomical interruptions was reached on the farm of C.W. Campbell near here when a meteorite crashed into the straw pile, set it afire, sent frightened horses galloping to distant fields.

The separator owner, S.A. Sanford, organized his bewildered men and the threshing machine was pulled to safety from the burning straw. A fire guard was hurriedly plowed to protect the stooked crop and buildings.[3]

## Hell's Wells

At one time, monsters other than the fire demon inhabited the prairie landscape. The lands of the ancient past, where dinosaurs roamed and lush plant life was abundant, are closely associated with modern-age, prairie hell fires. Long before the arrival of man, beds of coal and pools of petroleum formed where the prairies are now located. For the lurking demon, both have always been tempting sources of fuel.

Even before Hector observed fire smouldering in coal beds along prairie rivers, Native people knew that the surfaces of some sloughs would burn. In later years on the prairies, coal mine fires would take lives, and petroleum fires would also create great risks. Sometimes, the fires would even shift from the site of a well accident or blowout to the prairie fields nearby.

Early communities throughout Alberta and in the southern half of Saskatchewan were often at risk from petroleum-related fires. Historically, Alberta communities such as Longview, Turner Valley, Black Diamond, and Medicine Hat were frequently associated with images of oil and gas-related fires.

*The development of the petroleum industry increased the fire hazard on the prairies. Any fire involving a well site introduced the possibility of explosions and continuous, uncontrollable burning.* Glenbow Archives NC-26-325

These communities also suffered the usual fire hazards of short grass country: scant precipitation, strong winds, severe lightning storms, few natural fire barriers, and winter Chinooks that produced strong winds and reduced snow cover. Nitroglycerin and dynamite were also used and stored in the area. Early industry practices were poorly regulated, so gas leaks were common. High-pressure gas lines could also burst. Not surprisingly, explosions and fires became fairly common in the early history of the petroleum industry on the prairies.

In 1924, Royalite Number 4 blew out at Turner Valley. The well's pressure couldn't be controlled, and the well caught fire, burning for eleven days. The following year, the Freehold well at nearby Millarville was the site of a fire. In fact, it became the site of two fires. One month-long blaze started from a spark when someone changed a light bulb. The second resulted when a careless contractor dropped a match.

Black Diamond was the site of numerous fires. There, as in many early communities, the only available water was in the river. Without water service, the town depended on the Imperial Oil Company truck to haul water when the village was threatened by fire. The town did not purchase fire-fighting equipment until 1946.

Two years earlier, in 1944, a fire spread from an Okalata well to the near-by hamlet of Hartell. Many men from the community were away at war and others were at work when the women and children, living in shack-like homes at the work camp, found themselves in harm's way.

Strong winds carried the fire at lightning speed across the prairie grass. The fickle flames spared homes but levelled the church, garage, and pool-room. The fire jumped the highway, and before it was under control, eight farmers were left with blackened pastures and charred feed. Acknowledging that it was responsible for the fire, the Okalata Oil Company compensated farmers, but paid only half of the damages claimed by victims.[4]

One of the worst petroleum-related fires on the prairies happened on a farm in central Alberta, near Leduc. In 1948, the Leduc oil field made the headlines when Imperial Oil's Leduc Number 1 well blew in. In March, about 1 kilometre (0.6 miles) away, Canadian Atlantic Well Number 3 experienced a blowout. Soon, that wildcat well, located on John Rebus's farm, was infamous.

The fire story began when pressure broke the well seals. Efforts to reseal the well failed. One and a quarter million barrels of oil and billions of cubic metres of natural gas escaped the underground caverns. Once unleashed, petroleum geysers surfaced in numerous places around the wellhead.

To prevent the rest of the Leduc oilfield from being sucked into the blowout of well Number 3, oil men tried pumping mud down the drill hole. When that didn't work, they tried pumping water, cement, wheat, sawdust, golf balls, and feathers down the original drill hole and adjacent, newly drilled entry points. However, there was no stopping the blowout on John Rebus's farm.

Knowing the potential risk to his farm and family, Rebus ploughed wide fireguards. Both he and the oil company posted signs prohibiting the use of matches, pipes, and cigarettes in the area, but signs alone could not prevent foolishness or disaster.

A workman went to the outhouse, and deciding he needed a smoke, flicked his lighter. The explosion was instantaneous and caused a serious fire. Luckily, the workman was more frightened than hurt. However, soon after, sparks from the fire ignited the wellhead. Nicknamed Hell's Well by Edmonton journalists, the well became the centre of a raging inferno. Roaring on more than 16 hectares (40 acres) of land, the flames licked sky-ward, and smoke billowed 183 metres (600 feet) into the air. Although visi-ble from 64 kilometres (40 miles) away, the fire was eventually contained in the Rebus field.[5]

*In 1948, the fire at a Canadian Atlantic Oil Company well on the Rebus farm, near Leduc, Alberta, became one of the most difficult of all fires to extinguish on the prairies; the fire raged for six months.* Provincial Archives of Alberta, Kensit Studio Collection KS.66/5

The demon at Hell's Well was likely the most difficult of all fire demons to subdue in the West. The battle was not won until 9 September, more than six months after the fire had started. Unfortunately, the land that had fallen victim to the inferno took decades to be reestablished as productive farmland.

Less than a decade after the Leduc fire, a gas well blew out of control and caught fire 16 kilometres (10 miles) from the Saskatchewan border.[6] At first, workers tried the old method of forcing mud down the hole to choke off escaping gas, but that didn't work. Fortunately, emergency equipment had improved, and eventually, workers were able to use new equipment to reach into the flaming well and turn off valves. The flow of gas was halted, and the flames extinguished, but fire continued to lurk as an enemy near oil and gas fields, a circumstance that required those on the job to remain ever vigilant.

## Towers Aflame

Few visions can compete with the sight of grain elevators on fire—the prairies' towering infernos. Grain elevators form an integral part of the western economy. Most were built during the early settlement period, and in even the smallest town, usually two or more elevators lined railway tracks, symbolizing western prosperity.

Yet, from the time grain elevators were first built, these same symbols have gone up in flames, powerful reminders of the prairie fire story. Filled with thousands of bushels of grain, the elevators have fuelled inextinguishable fires that have threatened every building and every person living in prairie towns.

Like powder kegs, grain elevators provide perfect conditions for fire. The outside walls are built of wood. The huge buildings are located along railway tracks, where fuel may have spilled and soaked into the ground. On the bald prairie, the towers attract lightning. Inside is combustible dust and an endless fuel source. In the days before internal sprinklers became available, there was no way to get at a fire once it had started in the stored grain. Working from the outside was a futile task for fire fighters, since pumps could not force water to the elevators' high walls and roof.

Lining the railway tracks, numerous elevators could fall victim in the same holocaust. Many prairie towns have been threatened by elevator fires, and despite increased knowledge, suitable precautions, and modern equipment, elevators still catch fire.

On 4 October 1971, the townspeople of Penhold, Alberta, faced a grim struggle when two burning grain elevators threatened the existence of their community. At 1:00 AM on a Sunday morning, two older teens saw smoke near the town's four elevators; the second and fourth in the row were aflame. With the storage of the fall crop complete, both elevators were three quarters full. At the Alberta Wheat Pool elevator, 78,750 bushels of grain fuelled the flames. At the Federal, 48,750 bushels were in storage.

The town of 430 people could not afford its own fire department and depended on the nearby Red Deer Fire Department to rush to its aid. So, when the boys discovered the fire, they called Red Deer. One boy's mother also called neighbouring Innisfail and the Penhold Canadian Forces Base for help. Meanwhile, townspeople used buckets and garden hoses to battle the fire demon. Unable to do anything to halt the fire in the burning elevators, people fought frantically to save the other two elevators and the rest of their town.

Men from the air force base helped, and fire trucks arrived. The Innisfail Fire Department arrived twenty minutes after the call, and Red Deer fire fighters reached the scene within the next ten minutes. They beat out hot spots where they could, but the flames leaped more than 30 metres (100 feet) into the air. At times, the heat drove everyone away from the inferno.

*In 1971, these two grain elevators were levelled by fire in Penhold, Alberta.*
Provincial Archives of Alberta, *Edmonton Journal* Collection, J.5035/4

In the end, the Alberta Wheat Pool and Federal elevators were completely engulfed in flames. The collapse of their walls created showers of burning embers. Where once the Wheat Pool and Federal elevators had towered, there remained only two piles of burning grain and debris, glowing red against the night sky.

Flames licked repeatedly at the roof of the general store across the street, but there, townspeople managed to keep the enemy at bay. Fire burned a hole in the roof of a third elevator, the National, but again fire fighters managed to extinguish it. They also kept the United Grain Growers Elevator from bursting into flame.

Fortunately, homes and stores in Penhold had been spared from the flames, but the fire had been the third mysterious large fire to rage in three weeks. On 17 September, the United Grain Growers elevator and feed mill had gone up in flames at nearby Rocky Mountain House. Three days later, 30,000 bales of straw were destroyed by fire at a Red Deer farm.

According to RCMP officer Jack Roy, "Some things are just too much for coincidence. We will be investigating this [the Penhold fire] as if it were an arson."[7] Once again, in the land of fire, a terrible monster lurked.

# CHAPTER NINE

# Life Goes On

People who make the prairies their home have learned to live with prairie fire, the Destroyer. Sometimes several generations from a single farm family suffered its effects. Whereas in the past Mounties played a critical role in fighting fires, today the Mounties' role is restricted to serving and enforcing evacuation orders, and blocking roads to traffic unrelated to the firefighting effort. The RCMP can also conscript help for fighting fires, but few people ever dream of refusing a request for help.

## Fanning Flames into Friendship

Like all Westerners in the 1930s, the ranchers near Cochrane, Alberta, suffered the effects of drought and economic depression. Still, they were fortunate to live in one of the most spectacular prairie communities in the world. Their ranches were nestled in the foothills, and warm Chinook winds moderated the effects of winter. Around the ranches lay hogback ridges and vast expanses of grassland where cattle, sheep, and horses grazed. On the western horizon stood the spectacular Rocky Mountains.

The summer of 1936 had been long, hot, and dry, and by mid-November, only a dusting of snow covered the hills. On 18 November, the smoke from a small brush fire was visible in the forestry reserve to the west of Cochrane. The cause of the fire was unknown, but it was unlikely lightning so late in the season. The muskeg-like area of Jumping Pound Creek was also not especially prone to fire, but perhaps embers from an abandoned campfire had been fanned back into life.

By 1:00 AM on 19 November, flames engulfed the Sibbald Flats area. Then at about 4:00 AM, a single long ring on the party-line telephones signalled fire and raised the alarm for the entire community.

Men set out to help neighbours, but conditions were worse than expected. The wind had picked up, and strong men had to steady themselves along fence lines to make their way to barns and machine sheds. Those who rode horseback to the fire also battled the windstorm, which blew stones and debris against them and their mounts.

Such strong winds meant that fire would spread quickly and threaten numerous ranches. Some ranchers, including the Copithornes, who had been early settlers in the area, backfired to protect their property. Other ranchers put tractors into service, ploughing fireguards around their homes, barns, sheds, and haystacks. Unfortunately the equipment only moved at about 6 kilometres (4 miles) per hour, while the wind had reached gale-force strength.

Gusts were estimated at 151 kilometres (94 miles) per hour near the edges of the fire. They were likely stronger near the centre, where the fire created its own winds. The flames themselves reached speeds of about 96 kilometres (60 miles) per hour as they raced across expanses of grassland.[1]

Immediate evacuation was essential. Piled in wagons and Model A cars, most women and children were hurried to Jumping Pound Creek and Cochrane. However, earlier that morning, a group of children had left for school in nearby Brushy Ridge, before ranchers realized the full magnitude of the fire. Stranded without transportation, seventeen students and their teacher were in imminent danger, so two ranchers set out to save them.

By then, visibility was minimal. Even driving in the smoke-darkened landscape was risky. Without thought for themselves, the men made their way to the school, as the fire pressed closer and closer. They quickly evacuated the students and teacher from the schoolhouse, which was soon levelled by flames.

Others were also in grave danger. One pregnant woman had tried driving to Calgary, following a line of burning fence posts in the mid-day darkness. Suddenly, she came to a roadblock of debris deposited by the wind, so she quickly turned around and drove in the opposite direction. Finally, she reached Cochrane, where she sat out the ordeal.

Throughout the morning, volunteers fighting the fire waged a battle that remained beyond their control. In places, flames leapt 6 metres (20 feet) in the air. Powerless against the blaze, the best the men could do was urge their nervous horses and dogs to herd endangered livestock out of harm's way. When time ran out, ranchers and ranch hands simply opened gates and hoped their animals could outrun the fire. Sadly, many animals did not escape the flames, and losses were heavy.

The firestorm raged across 40,470 hectares (100,000 acres), leaving the land blackened and desolate. Those who had the time threw their posses-

*Following the Brushy Ridge fire of 19 November 1936, near Cochrane, Alberta, all that remained of the Arnell home was a levelled foundation and iron bedstead.* Glenbow Archives NB-16-647

sions down water wells for safekeeping, but at least twenty men, women, and children were left with little more than the clothes on their back. Of the seven families who were left homeless, two suffered enormous losses and five lost everything.

Despite the bravery of the people fighting the prairie fire, human effort did not bring victory this time. Only nature brought closure to the event at about 1:00 PM, when the winds subsided and rain extinguished the flames.

Albertans were steeped in the rural tradition of helping neighbours in trouble. Somehow, ranchers were surviving the economic stresses of the 1930s; they were also determined to not be destroyed by this devastating fire. Almost immediately, the *Calgary Herald* created the Bow Valley Fire Fund. The newspaper kicked off the campaign by donating $100, at a time when a good job might pay $2 per day, and when farm families on assistance received $10 per month. In little more than a week, the fire relief fund hit $3260. Donations continued to arrive from throughout the province, and additional special events in Calgary raised money for rebuilding. With the worst of winter looming, neighbours and volunteer carpenters from

Calgary, Cochrane, and Langdon worked tirelessly to build new homes for the homeless.

To assist the ranchers who no longer had feed for their remaining animals, the Western Stock Growers Association offered help. It arranged free transportation on the Canadian Pacific Railway to ship livestock to farms where feed was available. Some of those farms were as far north as the town of Olds, in central Alberta.

The blanket of snow on the prairie lay deep that year. Nevertheless, there were places where embers from the firestorm continued to smoulder until they were extinguished by the heavy rains of June 1937. That year brought bumper crops on the prairies, and the worst of the drought and economic depression ended, but memories of the fire remained.

At the time, southern Alberta was not considered at risk for cyclones or tornadoes. Yet, the winds that had fanned the 1936 fire were described as funnel-like formations blowing across the land. In the immediate vicinity of the fire, roofs had been blown from barns and other farm buildings. Equipment and debris had been lifted and then dropped by the winds. Even east of Calgary, telephone and power lines had been blown over. The pattern of damage suggested the foothills ranching community, where Chinook winds were familiar and welcome, had survived a wildfire carried on gale-force winds, quite possibly the winds of a cyclone.

## Thou Shalt Not

The farmers of Readlyn, Saskatchewan, were not people to defy the law. They lived by the rules, and in the 1940s, the rules prohibited using cheap purple farm gas for general transportation. Instead, the more expensive orange gas was to be used for this purpose. So, if a half-ton truck was driven on public roads, the farmer who filled it with purple was in hot water. Even so, exceptional circumstances could arise when a little purple in the tank could be a farmer's best friend.

Carl Claussen emigrated from Norway to Canada around 1927. He eventually married and settled on a farm near Readlyn. He and his hired man, Clarence Coldwell, were just being good citizens one day in the early 1940s when they jumped into Claussen's year-old truck and left to help fight a fire. Although it was the spring planting season, all farming was put on hold until the age-old fire enemy was defeated.

Flames, sparked by a CPR train, had spread near the farm owned by Claussen's father-in-law, burning a stretch almost 5 kilometres (3 miles) wide and 18 kilometres (11 miles) long. If the fire reached the grain elevators and Imperial Oil fuel tanks in town, the community would instantly become a disaster area. The foe had to be stopped.

Farmers brought their tractors and ploughs to fight the fire. Meanwhile, Claussen drove up and down the fire line, delivering men and equipment to where they were needed most. With his fuel tank nearly empty and disaster still looming, Claussen quickly filled up with the readily available purple gas and returned to the battleground. Everyone worked furiously, and in the end, the flames were extinguished.

Triumphantly, the hardworking Claussen stopped at the Co-op in town for a fill-up with orange gas. As he pulled in, the telltale black exhaust of purple gas trailed behind his truck. Clearly, Claussen had illegal gas in his tank.

Unfortunately for Claussen, highway traffic control was on the job that day, and his new truck was confiscated. The young farmer would have to pay the $70 fine before he could get his truck back. Losing his truck for two weeks during spring planting was not the reward Claussen had expected for being a good citizen and helping to save the town. However, Readlyn was located close enough to the RCMP training barracks that the rule of law prevailed.

Common sense dictates that Claussen should not have been fined for his crime. However, perhaps the hard-line officer who had fined him had missed the lesson on the outstanding role Mounties had once played in helping Westerners fight prairie fires. Most certainly, he had been absent for the lesson on discretion sometimes being the better part of law enforcement.

## Generations of Flames

Vast ranching and farming areas of the prairies were hit by flames again and again. Sometimes the owners of the land changed, but just as often generations within a family faced the same problems with fires. In fact, the mantle of fire fighter was often passed from father to son, and fire fighting was part of the shared experience that knit communities together.

One of the largest and earliest ranches in central Alberta was the Imperial Ranch near Big Valley. The vicinity suffered from fires in 1905 and 1906. Added to the devastation of the December 1906 fire was the hardship of a brutally cold winter and heavy snowfalls, which cost hundreds of cattle their lives.

John McAllister began building his own spread in the area after his arrival in 1907. Although he started with a homestead quarter, his operation grew steadily. Other nearby settlers included the Walters, Usher, Durkan, Dicemen, McKnight, and McCarty families. Over the years, they fought many blazes together, including an inferno in 1909 that threatened the range of the Walters, Ushers, and McAllisters. Despite the fires, many families were there to stay; others, who were in financial trouble for a variety of reasons, had to sell out.

About 1907, Pat Burns purchased the land and vast leases of the Imperial Ranch, which stretched across four townships and covered about 373 square kilometres (144 square miles). Yet, in terms of the Burns empire, the ranch was not financially viable, so he eventually sold the land and leases.

By 1917, John Walters and Tom and Charlie Usher had acquired most of what had once been Imperial land. The McAllisters also owned a huge spread that bordered the old Burns ranch, an area where fires would plague generations of their families.

One such fire occurred during the drought of the Dirty Thirties. On 14 April 1932, neighbour William White decided to burn some weeds and trash along the fence line bordering Usher pastureland. Suddenly the fire began to run, crossing two other farms and burning a hay field and granary. The shifting winds carried the fire west to the lease lands of the Ushers and Walters. There it blazed a swath more than 3 kilometres (2 miles) wide across three sections of land.

There were few cars and trucks available to bring help from Big Valley, but the McAllisters had hired a ranch crew of about a dozen men who suddenly had to become fire fighters. In all, about one hundred locals battled the blaze, including the McKnights, Durkans, Dicemens, Walters, and Ushers. The fire moved so quickly there was no time to pull equipment to the site of the fire for ploughing more guards. Instead, as in years past, the battle was waged by hand. Backfires were set in front of the main fire and quickly extinguished, creating a protective, fuel-free zone.[2]

Twelve-year-old Archie McAllister and Frances McKnight, a competent cattle woman, had the job of following the main line of fire fighters. They checked for smouldering embers and fires that had jumped the burned guard.

The blaze lasted almost three days, filling the sky with a lurid, red glow that was visible miles away. It was finally contained by a wide fireguard and doused the following week by record rainfalls in the area.

No human lives and no livestock were lost, but about 18 square kilometres (7 square miles) of hay land were charred. The Walters and the Ushers each lost about 544 to 635 tonnes (600 to 700 tons) of hay.[3] Despite the dev-

*In 1948, a vast area of grazing land was blackened during this fire, near Pat Burn's Bow Valley Ranch, just outside Calgary, Alberta.* Glenbow Archives, *Calgary Herald* Print File, Fires 1945-1959

astation, there was no compensation offered by the government. According to Archie McAllister, "you got what you got," and you did what you had to do. Even though the fire had been an accident, White was fined $125 and court costs.[4]

When it came to prairie fires, most rural people were like Archie McAllister. As the years passed, he continued to help fight blazes as an organizer, fire guardian, and patroller in the fire-prone land of his birth.

Fire-fighting efforts on farms and ranches would never benefit from the equipment, paid manpower, and funding of the fire departments being organized in towns and cities. In rural areas, the organization of fighting fires was much more fluid. Nevertheless, neighbours like the Walters, Ushers, McAllisters, and McCartys did develop their own successful systems and methods. They also had the good sense to know that saving a neighbour's grass and farm, no matter how far away, was often the only way to save one's own place.

In the early spring of 1946, another runaway fire hit the area. This time, from fifty to sixty locals arrived to help Tom McCarty save his hay and pastureland.[5] Someone asked Tom how the fire had started, but he had no idea. One man even said in an accusatory manner, with less than the usual neighbourliness, that if any of his land was burned, there would be hell to pay. Ironically, after the fire was extinguished, it was learned that it had started on the farm of the accuser. He had lit a bale of hay surrounded by snow to get rid of unwanted straw and had left it to burn. The wind lifted the burning debris, and the battle against the fire was on.

In 1949, lightning struck a fence and started still another fire. This one was on the Imperial Ranch lease land held by Walters. McCarty was among the fire fighters, and he made good use of his truck. Filling barrels of water at the trough in the Walters' corrals, McCarty delivered water for wetting the gunnysacks used to fight fires. By 10:00 PM, the fire seemed to be out, and everyone went home. Fortunately, McCarty had left the water barrels in his truck. Later, the flames reared back to life, and the battle had to be renewed until rain doused the fire.

The next year, exhaust from a vehicle in a stubble field was the culprit for starting yet another fire. Again, McCarty was among the fire fighters. This time "quite a few people [were] just spectators, like it was at a city building [on] fire [with] the firemen doing the work." The rainbow crowd, as McCarty called them, arrived after the firestorm was over. Before the year's end, the restless fire demon struck in the area again. A duck hunter who dropped a cigarette was believed to have started the blaze.

In 1962, the fire enemy leaped at another opportunity. A tractor had overturned on the old Imperial leases. A hay field caught fire, and a south wind swept the blaze ahead of it. Once again, about 1619 hectares (4,000 acres) of Usher land was blackened, as well as some of McCarty's pasture. In all, three haystacks were razed.

It was a McAllister whose life had been endangered in the blaze. Like many farmers, Lloyd McAllister had brought his tractor to help plough fireguards. Lloyd's tractor stuck on a rock in the path of the flames. Before he could escape, he was badly burned, and he spent days recovering at the Stettler hospital.

Like others in the area, Tom McCarty witnessed many fires. He also witnessed enormous changes as the Big Valley and Stettler areas grew from pioneer to twentieth century communities. Caring about the past, he began writing about local history.

On a summer day in 1976, McCarty decided to take a manuscript in for typing, and he put it in his truck. Though he had just bought the truck the year before, it backfired and sparked a blaze. After he and his neighbours had beaten the enemy into submission, they quaffed some beer to celebrate the victory. Then McCarty headed back to his truck.

I looked at the truck cab and there wasn't anything left but the steel and the seat spring. Oh, my God! My manuscript! My manuscript! I was pulling my hair and swearing blue streaks.

Although life in the fire belt was never easy, McCarty eventually received eighty percent of the price of his truck from the insurance company. The lost manuscript couldn't be replaced. However, McCarty did not allow the fire to claim the stories of his community's past, and he continued to write.

## The Madness Continues

After more than a century of fighting fires, prairie people still face wildfires, both in their communities and across the land that is their livelihood and their heritage. On 14 December 1997, southern Alberta again found itself face to face with an enemy of almost unimaginable power and intensity.

Throughout November and December, the southern prairies experienced some of the most pleasant early winter temperatures on record. The unseasonably dry weather and lack of snow were welcome, until a fire began on a farm in the Porcupine Hills area, about 120 kilometres (75 miles) south of Calgary.

Without snow cover, the Palliser Triangle was tinder dry. Making matters worse, the wind came up. With gusts reaching 50 kilometres (31 miles) per hour, the fire raged across the prairies. By 11:00 AM, it was clearly out of control. Huge clouds of smoke filled the sky, and the wind dropped ashes and embers as far away as Brooks.

The fire line spread for 25 kilometres (15 miles) across the horizon. People, homes, and livestock throughout the Granum–Pincher Creek area were endangered. As had been the case for more than a century, the Mounties played an important role in the fire response. They blocked roads to all but essential vehicles, notified farmers in the path of the fire, and evacuated those who needed help—even those who resisted evacuation. In the end, about half of the inhabitants of Granum were evacuated for their own safety, and as always, neighbours helped. Willow Creek Composite High School, in the neighbouring town of Claresholm, was turned into an emergency shelter for about sixty of the displaced victims.

The fire continued to rage, the smoke choked those near the inferno, and the sky rained tiny pieces of blackened debris. Some saw the fire from a perspective not possible earlier in prairie history. A newspaper reporter and a photographer were flown over the fire by pilot Lou Cattoni, who estimated that the smoke trail was from 70 to 80 kilometres (44 to 50 miles) long.[6] Others on the ground estimated the flames were visible 32 kilometres (20 miles) away, and some claimed smoke was visible 75 kilometres (47 miles) away.

Many in the area, including residents of the Peigan Indian Reserve, volunteered to fight the fire. Others herded about eight hundred head of livestock from enclosures, where death would otherwise have been a certainty. Men fighting the fire worked to exhaustion and only rested for a short time at the local hall, where women served them with sandwiches and coffee. Other helpful people drove to roadblocks, their cars packed with lunches for the fire fighters.

More than one hundred Hutterites lived in a local colony, a short distance from Granum. They were joined by another seventy-five Hutterites, from twenty Alberta colonies, for the fire-fighting effort. At the Granum colony, access to water was limited, so the non-resident Hutterites brought water trucks, as well as farm equipment. They were all set to work at clearing stubble from the path of the fire, ploughing fireguards, and spraying water on buildings. In the end, they could not stop the flames that claimed a barn, feed lot, and hay sheds.

For Stan and Clara Byers, the tragedy was almost beyond bearing. Since the turn of the century, the Byers family had farmed near Granum. Their farmhouse had been built in 1903, and Clara and Stan had lived there since the 1940s. When the fire first threatened, the Byers thought it was too far away to worry about. Then suddenly, the fire approached their farm. Stan, Clara, and their son, Jim, planned to leave in two separate vehicles. As Jim and Clara drove off, the fire was only 46 metres (150 feet) away. Desperately wanting to believe they would be spared, Stan couldn't tear himself away. At the last minute, the RCMP forced Stan to leave with them, "like a common criminal," he later lamented.[7]

Jim took Clara to a hotel at Claresholm. Then, avoiding the blockade, he used the back roads to return to the farm. In the end, the farm was reduced to a charred landscape. The Byers were glad their lives had been spared, but nothing could take away the pain of losing their farm and their heritage. "Yesterday, we were just sitting after lunch—not a worry in the world. Not a worry in the world. Now it's all gone forever."

The Big Coulee Ranch near Pincher Creek was also surrounded by fire. With three hundred head of cattle in the path of the fire, owner Phillip Kaiser, his ranch hands, and neighbours tried driving the livestock to safety. Panicking, the cattle turned back toward the fire. One neighbour attempted to head them off in his truck.

Two other neighbours, Derek and Bryan Heric, had also taken their

*Fire ravaged the prairie landscape in the Granum–Pincher Creek area from December 1997 to early 1998, during the winter of one of the strongest El Niño weather patterns on record. George Elgin's home was levelled in the fire just before Christmas. Born in the house, he had lived there throughout his seventy-two years. Here Wayne Zoeterman surveys the littered landscape that was once the Elgin home.* Calgary Herald, 16 December 1997.

truck to the area. They were searching for their mother and father, who had intended to cut a Christmas tree somewhere nearby. When Derek and Bryan noticed the problem with the cattle, they left their truck and helped herd the livestock. Still, on the Big Coulee Ranch, thirty to forty cattle were injured. One horse died in the fire; another was so badly injured it was put down. In all, ranchers lost at least 120 cattle during the fire.

Bryan and Derek Heric's parents had been trapped on the west side of the fire and were not able to get home. However, they had a cell phone with them and quickly let their sons know they were safe.

Phillip Kaiser's mother was less fortunate. At the time of the fire, eighty-year-old Frieda Kaiser was at her son's ranch. The large ranch house was built of brick. Still, it was not entirely safe from the inferno. Frieda had been able to get out of the flame-threatened house safely, but her dress caught fire. Her hands and feet were seriously burned, and she had to be flown to a Calgary hospital.[8]

Sadly, seventy-two-year-old George Elgin lost his home, the home in which he had been born. Robert and Cathy Day lost two hay barns, three sheds, hay, and a tractor, but the fire had skirted their house. To them, their good fortune was God's gift.

By late Monday night, fire fighters believed the worst was over. Then, the next day, the flames were again fanned into life. By midnight Tuesday, control had been re-established, although fire fighters kept a close watch on the area until 3:00 AM.

By the time it was stopped, the fire had blackened an estimated 53,000 acres (about 750 hectares) of valuable grazing land and left 3,000 to 5,000 cattle without winter feed. It also burned 6 bridges and 1,000 kilometres (621 miles) of fence.

In the tradition of prairie people helping each other in time of disaster, a Scorched Earth Band Aid Benefit Concert was held in Fort Macleod immediately after Christmas. People from around the province sent donations to the disaster fund. Come spring, retired farmers from as far away as Stettler, in central Alberta, intended to go fencing to help strangers in need.

The lessons of the past promised that the land would turn green once again, but the Granum–Pincher Creek fire will remain in people's memory as one of historic proportions.

# The Power of Place

In the West, fire has as much to do with place as it does with people. Fire danger is intrinsic to the prairie plains and parkland. Natural fire causes, as well as geographic and climatic risks, are ever present. Throughout hot summers, lightning bolts rivet earth to sky. The wind is a demon in its own right, fanning sparks into flames and lifting burning debris, to create havoc wherever it lands. Precipitation is scant; dry springs and autumns are ideal for the fire monster, and natural drought cycles accentuate the problems.

Little moisture and no snow cover was a crucial factor in the December, 1997, Granum–Pincher Creek fire in Alberta. That same weekend, seventeen other fires burned in Alberta.[1] The great El Niño and dry spring of 1998 brought more fires. By 21 April, sixty-three grass and bush fires were burning in Alberta, more than three times the number of fires reported by the same date the previous year.[2] The most devastating spring fire on the prairies occurred not in the Palliser Triangle but near Swan Hills, Alberta, about 200 kilometres (125 miles) north of Edmonton. There, vast forested lands were under attack, necessitating two evacuations of the community. However, just as the story of fire in the Palliser Triangle is not a new one, the story of forest fire on the prairies is also not new. The land of opportunity for thousands of early settlers has always been uniquely suited for the spread of fire, whether in the forests or parklands, or on the plains.

In addition to natural fire causes, there have always been others related to people. In the early days, homes and farms made use of technologies that themselves were fire prone. Settlers built their own homes, and often stovepipes and chimneys were defective or fit poorly. The warmest place to dry wet clothes was behind the kitchen stove; when dry, the clothes hanging

*This fire started on 8 September 1906 in a restaurant at Lacombe, Alberta. Sparked by overheated furnace pipes, it destroyed most of the block.* Glenbow Archives ND-2-61

there became a fire hazard. Gas and coal oil lamps were also accidents waiting to happen.

In the settlement years, children had tremendous and dangerous responsibilities, at very young ages. They lit stoves and lamps. They cooked meals and burned garbage. They helped burn virgin land, weed patches, and stubble. As well-intentioned as they might be, they were still children. Today, the idea of combining childhood and fire is unthinkable, though at times, real life reminds us that these lethal combinations still occur.

Other things have also changed. The invention of light bulbs meant the long, dark nights could be safely lit. Nevertheless, such developments as gas appliances, plastics, and chemicals mingled safety and hazard. Fortunately, today, towns, cities, and municipalities have strict fire prevention laws.

Farming methods have also changed. Most virgin land has been cleared, so in recent years, fire has rarely been used for that purpose. Modern equipment makes cultivating easier. To maintain moisture and fibre in the soil, and to prevent wind erosion, stubble is often ploughed under rather than burned. Herbicides are commonly used for weed control, rather than burning weed patches.

The few operating steam locomotives that cross the prairies are a precious reminder of the past. However, they no longer endanger the landscape by belching sparks and dumping ashes along prairie rails.

Although most modern fires take place in towns and cities, often the result of accident or carelessness, well-trained and efficient fire departments usually extinguish them successfully. Methods of fighting wildfires have also evolved. To reduce fire risk, planned burns clear thick mats of natural grasses, leaves, needles, and other debris that otherwise would readily fuel fires.

Prevention and immediate response to alarms have been the most important factors in reducing fire-related tragedies and losses. With larger populations, better transportation, new communication technologies, and increased air traffic, flames are quickly spotted and extinguished.

Nevertheless, fires still rage uncontrolled within communities and across vast, open spaces. The ruin and anguish they cause are as distressing now as they were in ages past. During one of the spring fires of 1998, residents of DeWinton, Alberta, fought with rakes and shovels. According to one victim, "it was all smoke and flames were licking and going like hell."[3]

Westerners continue to battle the prairie fire demon and face the hardship and tragedy left in its wake. By allowing small ironies to put a smile on their faces, despite their losses, and by sharing stories of heroism and pain, prairie people have learned to live in the land where fires are legendary.

*Today, fire damage to prairie landscape is commonly viewed from the air. This aerial photograph shows fire devastation on the Blood Reserve in southern Alberta on 26 August 1973.* City of Lethbridge Archives and Records Management P19871019000

# *Notes*

## Introduction

1. Henry Youle Hind, Narrative of *The Canadian Red River Exploring Expedition of 1857 and the Assiniboine and Saskatchewan Exploring Expedition 1858* (Edmonton, AB: M.G. Hurtig Ltd., 1971), 336.
2. Captain John Palliser, *The Journals, Detailed Reports, and Observations Relative to the Exploration by Captain Palliser of a Portion of British North America* (London: George Edward Eyre and William Spottiswoode, 1863), A4. For further treatment on fires observed by the Palliser Expedition, see Chapter 1.
3. *Keeper of the Flame* (Ottawa, ON: Canadian Parks Service, 1989), 3–6. All references to this study are from this source.
4. W.F. Lothian, *A Brief History of Canada's National Parks* (Ottawa, ON: Environment Canada, Parks, 1987), 79. The proposal called for a park that would eventually cover 906.5 square kilometres in southwest Saskatchewan.
5. *Canadian Normals: Precipitation 1941–1970*, Volume 2–SI (Downsview, ON: Environment Canada, 1975), 58–65. All references to precipitation are from this source.
6. *Edmonton Journal*, 21 May 1998.
7. *Canadian Normals: Temperature, 1941–1970*, Volume 1–SI (Downsview, ON: Environment Canada, 1975), 32–40. All references to temperature are from this source.

## Chapter One. Land of Fire

1. Fred Yellow Old Woman, interview with the author, 18 June 1998.
2. Hind, *The Canadian Red River*, 337.
3. Ibid., 405.
4. Duncan McGillivray, as quoted from Arthur S. Morgan (editor), *The Journal of Duncan McGillivray of the North-west Company at Fort George on the Saskatchewan 1794–95* (10 October 1795), 30, in *Research Bulletin, National Historic Parks and Sites Branch*, no. 45 (Ottawa, ON: Parks Canada, Department of Indian and Northern Affairs, February, 1977), 3.
5. McGillivray, *Research Bulletin*, 5.
6. Palliser, *The Journals, Detailed Reports, and Observations*, 57–65. All references to the Palliser Expedition are from this source.
7. Earl of Southesk, *Saskatchewan and the Rocky Mountains* (Edinburgh: Edmonston and Douglas, 1875), 19.
8. Sir William Francis Butler, *The Wild North Land* (Toronto, ON: The MacMillan Company of Canada, Ltd., 1910), 50.

## Chapter Two. Lurking Enemies

1. David Cruise and Alison Griffiths, *The Great Adventure: How the Mounties Conquered the West* (Toronto, ON: Penguin Books Canada Ltd., 1997), 118.
2. Henri Julien, Diary entry for 16 July, as quoted by Marjorie Mason in *One Hundred Years of Grasslands* (North Battleford, SK: Turner-Warwick Publications, Inc., 1993), 24. Cruise and Griffith suggest the same entry was for 17 July, but other sources suggest the fire may have been 18 July.

3. John Macoun, *Manitoba: History of the Great Northwest* (Guelph, ON: The World Publishing Company, 1882), 651–653. Both quotes are from this source. Macoun's employment history is in the Preface.

4. As quoted from *The Macleod Gazette* in *Fort Macleod-Our Colorful Past* (Fort Macleod, AB: Fort Macleod Book Committee, 1977), 37.

5. Kenneth Coates and William R. Morrison, *My Dear Maggie: Letters from a Western Manitoba Pioneer, William Wallace* (Regina, SK: Canadian Plains Research Centre, University of Regina, 1991), 71–73. All references to the Wallaces and the fire are from this source.

6. [?] McKenzie, "A Prairie Fire," *Frontier and Pioneer Life, Prairie Fires* File, 3. Regional Public Library, Regina, SK. All references to this fire are from this source.

7. Fred Yellow Old Woman, interview with the author, 19 June 1998. Some details are taken from the retelling of the story to the author by Clifford Crane Bear, 18 June 1998.

### Chapter Three. A Range Ablaze 1880–1900

1. John Hawkes, *The Story of Saskatchewan and Its People*, vol. II (Regina, SK: The S.J. Clarke Publishing Company, 1924), 1090.

2. Col. S.B. Steele, *Forty Years in Canada* (Toronto, ON: McClelland, Goodchild & Stewart Ltd., c. 1918), 258–259.

3. Captain Burton Deane, *Mounted Police Life in Canada: A Record of Thirty-One Years' Service* (London: Cassell & Co. Ltd., 1916), 300. See also Deane, *Pioneer Policing*, 9, for information on this fire.

4. Daily Journal, Fort Macleod, RCMP Archives, 972.55.75, 17–27 September 1889.

5. Foothills Historical Society, *Chaps and Chinooks: A History West of Calgary* (Calgary AB: Northwest Printing & Lithographing Ltd., 1976), 273.

### Chapter Four. Wooden Towns

1. Vince Leah, *Alarm of Fire: 100 Years of Firefighting in Winnipeg 1882–1928* (Winnipeg, MB: Firefighters Burn Fund, 1982). See 52–83 for information regarding all Winnipeg fires mentioned in this treatment.

2. Edith Patterson, *Tales of the Early West* (Canada: Hignell Printing Ltd., 1978), 67–68.

3. *Regina Queen City of the Plains 1903–1953* (Regina, SK: Western Printers Association, 1955), 49.

4. Grant MacEwan, *100 Years of Smoke, Sweat and Tears* (Calgary, AB: Calgary Fire Department, 1984), 2.

5. George R. Provost, *Calgary 100: Calgary Centennial Souvenir Book* (Calgary, AB: Provost Promotions & Publications, 1974), 142.

### Chapter Five. Methods and Madness

1. *Annual Report of the Department of Agriculture of the North-West Territories*, 1903 (Regina, SK: John A. Reid, Government Printer, 1904), IX. This appears to be the 1904 fire Hugh Dempsey referred to in *The Golden Age of the Canadian Cowboy*, (Calgary, AB: Fifth House Publishers, 1995) 83.

2. *Annual Report of the Department of Agriculture of the North-West Territories*, 1904 (Regina, SK: John A. Reid, Government Printer, 1905), IX.

3. Lyalta, Ardenode, Delroy Historical Society, *Along the Fire Guard Trail: A History of Lyalta, Ardenode, Delroy Districts* (Calgary, AB, 1979), 1. All references to the Fireguard Trail are from this source.

4. *The Wilkie Press*, 10 September 1909. See also *The Wilkie Press*, 3 September 1909.
5. Clyde Leavitt, *Forest Protection in Canada* (Toronto, ON: Bryant Press, 1913), 1–4. All references to details of railway legislation are from this source.
6. "Fire! Fire!," *Lethbridge News*, 30 March 1892.
7. *Lethbridge News*, 16 December 1907. Reprinted in *Lethbridge: A Century of Fire Fighting* by Alex Johnston and Ted Bochan (Lethbridge, AB: City of Lethbridge Fire Department, 1986), 27.
8. *Mosquito Creek Roundup: Nanton-Parkland* (Calgary, AB: Nanton District Historical Society, 1975), 95.
9. Ibid., 95.
10. *Lethbridge Daily Herald*, 12 May 1910.

**Chapter Six. In Harm's Way**
1. Marjorie Wilkins Campbell, *The Silent Song of Mary Eleanor* (Saskatoon, SK: Western Producer Prairie Books, 1983). All references to this fire are from this source.
2. Konrad Istrati, *Virgin Sod: Opening & Settling the Prairies of Southern Saskatchewan* (Assiniboia, SK: Konrad C. Istrati, 1986), 305–309. All references to this fire are from this source.
3. Barry Broadfoot, *The Pioneer Years 1895–1914* (Toronto, ON: Doubleday Canada Limited, 1976), 70–72.
4. Jean James, "The Terrible Fire of 1909," *The Western Producer*, 6 July 1972. There are discrepancies between James's account of the fire and Campbell's account. See Note 6 below. These relate to the exact date of the fire and whether Mrs. Burress took both her children to the Grovers' or only Herbie, while Edward went with his father.
5. James, C3.
6. Marie Campbell, ed., *Still God's Country: The Early History of Byemoor and Area* (Altona, MB: Byemoor Historical Book Committee, 1975), 12–13.
7. *The Village That Grew: A History of North Red Deer* (Red Deer, AB: 75 Anniversary Committee, 1987), 103.
8. "The Brandon Asylum Fire of 1910," *Gazette, Manitoba History* (Spring 1991). For full discussion of the fire, see 17–20.

**Chapter Seven. Childhood with the Fire Demon**
1. Stephen Wilk, editor-in-chief, *100 Years of Nose Creek Valley History* (Calgary, AB: Nose Creek Historical Society, 1997), 79–81.
2. E.L. Lifeso, "Fighting prairie infernos," *Western People*, 21 February 1980, 14. All references to the fires affecting the Lifeso family are from this source.
3. Olive Fredeen, "The Prairie fire," *Western Producer*, 2 January 1975.
4. H. Holden, "Prairie fire," *The Western Producer*, 6 January, 1977. All references to this fire are from this source.
5. Philip Long, *The Great Canadian Range* (Vancouver, BC: Cypress Publishing Ltd., 1970), 160–161. All references to this fire are from this source.

**Chapter Eight. The Unexpected: Cause and Consequence**
1. Robert Hill, *Manitoba: History of Its Early Settlement, Development and Resources* (Toronto, ON: William Briggs, 1890), 449–487. All references to the fires in Portage la Prairie at this time are from this source.
2. Vince Leah, *Pages from the Past* (Winnipeg, MB: *The Winnipeg Tribune*, 1975), 94.

3. *Moose Mountain Star-Standard*, 30 October 1935.

4. *In the Light of the Flares* (Turner Valley, AB: Sheep River Historical Society, 1979), 114. All other references to Black Diamond, Longview, Hartwell, and Turner Valley are also from this source.

5. Grant MacEwan, *Coyote Music and Other Humorous Tales of the Early West* (Calgary, AB: Rocky Mountain Books, 1993), 105–107.

6. "Gas Well Fire Under Control," *Calgary Herald*, 25 October 1956.

7. *Red Deer Advocate*, 4 October 1971. All references to this fire are from this source.

**Chapter Nine. Life Goes On**

1. Foothills Historical Society, *Chaps and Chinooks: A History West of Calgary* (Calgary AB: Northwest Printing & Lithographing Ltd., 1976), 25–28. See also 420, 541, 597. All references to this fire are from this source.

2. Archie McAllister, taped interview with Ruby Reineberg, 6 February 1997. Also taped interview with Faye Holt, 20 March 1997.

3. *Stettler Independent*, 30 April 1932.

4. Ibid.

5. Tom McCarty, Untitled Notes Regarding Fires, April 1998. Copy held by the author. All references to the fires affecting Mr. McCarty are from this source.

6. *Calgary Herald*, 15 December 1997.

7. Ibid. See also *Calgary Herald*, 16 December 1997.

8. *Calgary Sun*, 16 December 1997. See also 15 December 1997.

**Afterword**

1. *Calgary Herald*, 15 December 1997.

2. *Calgary Herald*, 22 April 1998.

3. *Calgary Herald*, 22 April 1998.

# *Index*